REKHA KALINDI was born into a poor family in a village in West Bengal in 1997. From a young age she was obliged to give up her education to work and help bring in money to feed her family. Going back to school with the assistance of the Indian National Child Labour Project, she became a model pupil. However, at the age of eleven her parents said they had found her a husband. She staunchly opposed this, flying in the face of age-old custom and bringing her into conflict with her family. Only through the intervention of her teachers and the Minister of Labour of West Bengal was she able to continue her schooling. Since her story became known she has become a voice for millions of young people in India denied the opportunity to receive an education and have a proper childhood. She now travels all over India to speak, and her international profile continues to grow. Her story was one of only twenty (that of Anne Frank and Malala Yousafzai were two others) included in a book called, in English, *Children Who Changed the World* published to mark the twenty-fifth anniversary of the United Nations Declaration of the Rights of the Child, and she is the recipient of India's National Bravery Award.

MOUHSSINE ENNAIMI is a distinguished correspondent for Radio France, widely acknowledged as a specialist on India. His posting to South Asia led to a meeting with Rekha Kalindi and their collaboration on this book.

THE STRENGTH TO SAY NO

THE STRENGTH
TO SAY NO

ONE GIRL'S FIGHT AGAINST
FORCED MARRIAGE

Rekha Kalindi
with Mouhssine Ennaimi

Translated from the French by
Sarah Lawson

Peter Owen
London and Chicago

PETER OWEN PUBLISHERS
81 Ridge Road, London N8 9NP

Peter Owen books are distributed in the USA and Canada
by Independent Publishers Group / Trafalgar Square
814 North Franklin Street, Chicago, IL 60610, USA

Translated from the French *La Force de dire non*

First published in English by Peter Owen Publishers 2015
Reprinted 2015

© Éditions Michel Lafon 2012
English translation © Sarah Lawson 2015
Photographs (cover and plates) © Mouhssine Ennaimi

PAPERBACK ISBN 978-0-7206-1792-4
EPUB ISBN 978-0-7206-1829-7
MOBIPOCKET ISBN 978-0-7206-1830-3
PDF ISBN 978-0-7206-1831-0

A catalogue record for this book is available from the British Library

Typeset by Octavo Smith Publishing Services

Printed and bound in the UK by
CPI Group (UK) Ltd, Croydon, CR0 4YY

PREFACE

Arranged marriages are extremely widespread in Indian society, and these arranged unions frequently merge into forced marriages. This ancient cultural tradition then produces forced marriages that deprive the young couple of their individual liberty in flagrant violation of the rights of man and of the child according to the United Nations and Unicef. More than 40 per cent of the forced marriages in the world take place in India. This is a national curse that the authorities are trying to root out.

In spite of a clear and precise legislative arsenal (the Child Marriage Restraint Act of 1929 – popularly known as the Sarda Act) traditions are tenacious: girls and boys are always subject to their parents' decisions from the moment that their marriage comes up for discussion. The main motivations that drive parents to choose the future wife or husband of their children are respect for caste and social class, the patronymic and dynastic line and economic considerations. These arrangements are sometimes made without the children ever having met one another, or when they have met only briefly. The minimum legal age for marriage is eighteen for women and twenty-one for men, but this is ignored, neglected and sometimes not known, even by the privileged classes.

Children who are sometimes married off for reasons of economic survival (one less mouth to feed) are deprived of their liberty, separated from their friends, isolated from the rest of their family and forced to abandon their schooling. As for health, such children are more likely to be exposed to sexually transmitted diseases. A pregnancy during teenage years or earlier incurs the risk of causing serious after-effects on the female reproductive organs and the death of the infant and its mother during childbirth. The risk of death for the baby is 60 per cent greater when the mother is under the age of eighteen (source: United Nations). In India two out of five women are married before the legal age, and one in five before the age of fifteen. Furthermore the figures apply to all the childbirths in the population regardless of caste or education (source: 'The Situation of Children in India in June 2011', Unicef).

Of course, Rekha Kalindi did not know these statistical data any more than she knew that the rate of infant mortality in India is one of the highest in the world (higher than that in sub-Saharan Africa). However, her personal experience convinced her that an early marriage inevitably means damage to a girl's health as well as exclusion from the school system.

Mouhssine Ennaimi

CONTENTS

LIST OF ILLUSTRATIONS

between pages 64 and 65

All photographs by Mouhssine Ennaimi

Rekha Kalindi was just eleven years old when she met former Indian president Pratibha Singh Patil

Rekha helps her father rolling traditional Indian cigarettes (bidis); his low wage is barely enough to feed the family.

A young Bengali girl carrying wood

Rekha's mother was not supportive of Rekha at first and beat and starved her daughter when she refused to marry.

Rekha cycling through her home village of Bararola

Rekha's father with his drums – he occasionally plays in religious festivals and political marches to earn a little more money to support his family.

Rekha and all her family in Bararola village

Rekha's teacher, Atul, a key character in her life, who supported her when she refused to marry and encouraged her to continue to attend school

Josna, Rekha's older sister, who suffered greatly when she
became a mother at just twelve years old so influencing
Rekha's determination to defy her parents' wishes
for her to be married off at eleven

Rekha and her mother

Rekha at the door of her sister Josna's home

Rekha visiting a school to speak her of experiences and
how children facing the same situation should
question tradition and expectations

A teacher congratulates Rekha following a talk at a school

1

MEETING THE PRESIDENT

We were warned from the moment we went in. Don't look her in the eye, don't try to approach her and, most of all, be polite. This person, who I didn't even know existed until a few days ago, is the most important and the most respected person in the country. I could hardly believe that it could be a woman and furthermore that she wanted to meet me.

We go through the gardens before getting to the marble porch. We arrive in a luxurious room in which the carved walls are inlaid with symmetrical patterns. My new sandals slip on the white marble floor. I hitch up my long scarf-like *dupatta* so that I won't trip over it. The route we take is lined with pillars as big around as elephants' legs. The golden patterns of the mosaics sparkle from the combined reflection of sunlight and lit lamps. I fix my eyes on the doorway opposite to avoid being dazzled by all this light. I have never seen such a beautiful residence. Two armed guards stand motionless in front of our passage without, however, taking their eyes off us.

We cross a patio where we are received by several members of the security guard wearing uniforms of dark-grey shirts and trousers. One of the bodyguards speaks in Hindi into a walkie-talkie. I understand only part of the exchange. The women are called into an adjacent room. The women security guards in dark grey search us one by one. They ask us if we have electronic objects, pens or any other accessories in our possession. I reply politely in the negative. The frisking is embarrassing, and I glance at my friends and smile to make light of this ordeal. We get through a gate and find ourselves again on the patio. The men are put through the same treatment. Cameras and mobile phones are confiscated. My father is given a more rigorous search than the others. I go towards him, but the guards ask me to stay to one side. They have found some bidis – little cigarettes hand-rolled in a eucalyptus leaf – in my father's pockets. Although he maintains that he has no matches the guards search for anything that could produce fire, but in vain. The man takes up his walkie-talkie again to talk to his colleague. I gather that we can go on.

The floor is covered with a thick carpet with a floral pattern. There is no longer any risk that I'll slip. On the contrary, my sandals catch on it and now I have to be careful not to lose them. I look at the chandeliers hanging from the ceiling and I think to myself that they must weigh as much as a cow. The table in the middle is spread with a brilliant white tablecloth that almost touches the floor. Light-blue ribbons encircle the backs of the chairs. A man is standing behind each of the covered dishes. We are told that after we've met the president we can eat as much as we like. As I cross the room I notice that the vegetarian dishes are separated from the dishes with meat: the two buffet tables are several metres apart. We walk through umpteen rooms, one after the other. I wonder how many people live in this house.

Other guards are posted in front of a door made of dark, shiny wood. These men are wearing a different outfit, red and white, and they are not armed, unlike the ones who have been accompanying us since the beginning and who searched us meticulously. There are several double doors – to the right, the left and straight ahead. Each one of them is guarded by men wearing yet another uniform. There is a large chair, a microphone and several rows of smaller chairs. The guards talk to my parents, as well as to the people from the National Child Labour Project (NCLP) who supervise us in Purulia.

'There is a protocol, and you must respect it to the letter,' our tutor informs us. 'You mustn't speak to her before she addresses you, nor go too close to her, nor look her in the eye. You must not touch her feet as you're used to doing with your parents or your teachers. Confine yourself to a simple and respectful hello in Hindi – *namaste*. Also don't forget that you must wait until she is seated and tells you to sit. Pay attention and never interrupt her, and don't forget to say "ma'am" after anything you say to her.'

I look at my friends Afsana and Sunita. They look tense. My father is squeezed into his jacket and doesn't seem very relaxed either. There are a lot of people in the room – other people that I don't know – and most of them are wearing suits and ties. There are journalists and some of them have made the trip with us from Purulia. Prosenjit, our tutor, comes up and reminds us that we have to have perfect manners in front of the president. He seems to be nervous and overexcited at the same time.

The door opens, and I finally see the person I've been hearing about non-stop for several days. She is Pratibha Patil, the first woman president of India (from 2007 to 2012) and before that the first woman governor of Rajasthan. She has a nice face, little glasses and undoubtedly one of the most beautiful saris that I have ever seen. She is followed very closely by four armed men responsible for her protection. She comes up to me, and I put my hands together and bow my head. The president puts her hand on my shoulder.

'What's your name?'

'Rekha. Rekha Kalindi, ma'am.'

'I am very proud of you and very proud to meet you,' she says, taking my hand in both of hers.

'Thank you very much, ma'am,' I say, moved and nervous at the same time. I don't even think to tell her that I am honoured and proud to meet her in this palace.

'You are an example to a whole generation and for millions of girls . . .' The president speaks to me without this famous protocol that has been drummed into me from the beginning. She strokes my hands, while all the time looking me in the eye. I thank her for welcoming us in this house, and she smiles.

When she gets to Sunita and Afsana she just joins her hands to greet them. They have a brief conversation, and she thanks them for coming so many miles to be in New Delhi today. The president also greets my father, the mothers of my friends and the rest of the NCLP personnel. When she is seated we sit down, too.

The president tells us that she read our story in the local papers. She couldn't believe her eyes. 'Some girls have succeeded where government policy has been failing for thirty years.' She asked local staff to find out more about us. Ever since she received the findings and the confirmation of our experiences she was eager to meet us. I believe that she really meant it when she described us as heroines.

'We can make all the laws and all the modifications in our society that we like, but these initiatives in which we believe deeply are of no use if there aren't people like you. Our proposals are directed at people with characters like yours, and it is you, my girls, who are doing the most difficult work. Your courage has guided you to good decisions, and I am proud to see that the future generations of Indians are daring and ambitious. What you have done is exceptional. I am hopeful and sure that you will be an inspiration to other young girls. So that our country can eliminate this notion of marriage between two children at the cost of their education, their future and ultimately their happiness. I asked to see just one girl, but receiving three makes me still happier and prouder to represent our great country.'

The president hands over to our tutor, Prosenjit, and he asks us to rise. Afsana, Sunita and I thank the president for giving us such a great honour. Prosenjit briefly describes my situation, then that of Afsana and of Sunita. Other speeches follow from the men in suits and ties. Each one explains at what point his role was crucial in our lives and our choices, including some that I absolutely don't know. I look at the president, and she smiles at me. I had never thought that a woman could achieve this degree of responsibility nor receive so much deference from men. In my village in Bengal a girl remains inferior to a boy. A woman submits to the commands of her husband. The president says that I inspire her, but she is mistaken. She is the one who inspires us.

I blush when I think of my reaction a few days ago when I learned that she wanted to meet me. Prosenjit called the headmaster of my school, Arjun, who himself telephoned Arvind, the grocer in Bararola, the 'telecommunications centre' of my village. I remember that he was talking fast, short of breath as if he had forgotten that he had to breathe.

'Rekha, I have an amazing piece of news. The president wants to meet you!'

'Who?'

'The president in person. She wants to see you and no doubt congratulate you. You're going to go to New Delhi!'

'I don't know who you're talking about . . . Anyway, I'm not interested.'

'Don't talk like that, Rekha! Even if you don't know who she is, you owe her respect. She is one of the most important people in India.'

'Well, let me think about it. It's not like I have to decide instantly. Give me some time to think it over.'

'I'm going to Purulia to get the letter, and I'll show it to you tomorrow at school. It's incredible, a chance like this. You can tell your parents. I'm sure they'll be thrilled.'

'All right. See you tomorrow.'

And I hung up the phone.

How could I have been such an idiot? People don't say no to the president of their country. Now that I'm standing in front of her I'm sorry I lacked respect for her.

Arjun showed me the letter. The design on it was the same as the one that you see at the post office and in front of the offices of the NCLP. Later I found out that it is the coat of arms of all India.

The next day journalists phoned constantly. Some local elected officials hoped to meet me before I left for New Delhi.

Some even came to the house to greet me personally. The members of the NCLP talked of nothing but this visit to the president. I understood that it was a matter of incredible importance, and that in spite of the obstacles the reprimands and the insults of the past, I had made the right decision.

The president rose and left the room, always surrounded by the four armed men. The government officials congratulated me one by one. The journalists asked me the same questions as usual. Then it was time to go to lunch.

2
SCHOOL

'When a girl is born it's always bad news!' How many times have I heard this statement without really realizing that it concerns me? My father, my mother, everyone around me is convinced of it. I know that because I have often heard their conversations with the neighbours and other members of the family about female babies. It must be said that in my case my coming into the world really was bad news for my parents.

Even when I was a small child the list of faults attributed to me was already long: unruly and stubborn, persistent and difficult. Like other little girls I will lose my family name once I am married, and my parents will have to go into debt to be able to pay a dowry to the family of my future husband. I will not be able to cremate my father when he dies because only sons are involved in the cremation that is performed so that the father can attain the final liberation. All the fruits of my labour will go to my in-laws. It is not impossible that this will change in the future, but for now that's how things stand in India and in particular in the villages like the one in which I was born and where I live, where these traditions are solidly rooted in custom. As a little child I upset my father's tobacco pots and spoiled his work when I had the chance. In addition, they told me over and over, I had weakened my mother considerably. Breast-feeding wore her out to such an extent that she could no longer take care of the house as the other women in the village did.

From a very early age I realize that life will be difficult. My father, my Baba, rolls cigarettes all day long. It's his livelihood, as it is for most of the inhabitants of the village. Here everyone is linked in one way or another to the cigarette industry – men, women, grandparents and teenagers. Every week Baba carefully notes in a little notebook the amount of tobacco and the number of eucalyptus leaves delivered by the producer. From the first glimmers of sunlight my father sets up shop on the doorstep with his basket and arranges his work kit. Indoors everyone is still asleep, crowded together on straw pallets or even on the dried-mud floor near the few battered cooking utensils. At the end of the day Baba will have rolled nearly eight hundred bidis. I like to get up early and watch him do it. He began very young. I want him to teach me.

'You have to cut up the leaves – they ought to be the same size as this little iron plate,' whispers my father as he cuts the leaf with long black scissors.

'That's so you don't waste the rest?'

'Exactly! Sometimes you can make three cigarettes with one leaf. But most often you make two. Then you put just the right amount of tobacco, always with the idea of making it as profit-able as possible. The more bidis you make with the same small amount of material the more money you earn.'

Baba takes up a pinch of tobacco, lays the right amount on the eucalyptus leaf then puts the rest back in the basket. The next movement of his fingers seems automatic. In a few seconds my father has rolled the cigarette, circled it with a fine thread, packed down the top and folded the bottom. The cigarettes are arranged in packets of twenty-five at one side of the basket. He takes a second leaf with his right hand while the left grabs some tobacco.

'Can I do it too?'

My father continues his mechanical movements as he replies, 'Not now. I have to hurry because in the morning you work best and quickest. When I've finished you can practise. But pay close attention and don't waste the tobacco.'

These last few years Baba's abilities have greatly diminished. Since he is sitting down all day he has pains in his back and cramps that make him stop for several hours. His eyesight is also failing and his productivity suffers because of it. But this work by itself is not enough. To meet our needs when the occasion presents itself Baba goes to make some extra money at demonstrations organized by the communists by warming up the crowd with his drum. At other times he is employed as a porter or day worker in the rice paddies. The work is hard but it pays better.

I spend most of my days in the little courtyard in front of our house. I play jacks with stones and sometimes marbles or hopscotch with my friends and neighbourhood children. I did go to the village school, but when I was four my parents stopped sending me there. I learned to count up to ten, but only in Bengali – English isn't taught until much later. I am afraid I'll never have the chance to learn any more. From then on I help Ma to tidy up and clean our home. I also help her cook, at least when there's any food. It is not unusual for us not to have much to eat. I've got used to eating very little in order to leave more for my younger brothers and sisters or for Baba so that he can work. Lately the situation is very bad. Ma nurses my little brother Swapan, but she is not well. My father can't afford to send her to a doctor in town. The one in the village is the only one who has listened to her chest, but the medication he provided hasn't changed anything. Ma is always in a bad mood, and her pain is increasingly severe. The only solution is just to wait for it to go away.

We no longer have anything to eat. For several weeks now we have had to make do with one meal a day. My young brothers and sisters have empty bellies and often cry. The conversations between my parents end in arguments. Ma reproaches my father for not bringing in enough money to feed the whole family, forcing him to beg for rice from the neighbours. He is ashamed of it, but it is the only way for his children to have their next meal. The people of the village know our situation and give what they can out of solidarity. We are of the same caste, the same community and the same village.

During the day I help my father roll cigarettes so that he can earn more money. I take his place when he has cramps or when his back hurts too much. I make the same movements he does, but I don't have his endurance. I get tired very quickly after rolling a few hundred bidis.

My big sister Josna found work in a brick factory. The conditions there are very hard. She sleeps there, and when she comes home she tells us that she has trouble breathing. She inhales toxic fumes all day and also complains of back pains, but she would not quit the job for anything in the world. Without her wages we wouldn't be able to live.

One morning Ma asks me to go to the fields of the Mahatos, a rich family of landowners in Bengal. It's about an hour away on foot. I go cross-country, and I'm afraid of coming across snakes. I'm terrified of reptiles, and I know that their bites can be fatal. Several villagers have already been bitten by cobras.

I arrive at the rice paddy at around seven o'clock. The heat is still bearable. I go to meet the owner, and he confirms that he needs workers, especially at this time of the year when it's very hot during the day. I have to pull up the tall grass that is choking out the rice plants. I say to myself that if my parents had not had so many children they would be able to provide for themselves without having to beg from the neighbours. I have the feeling that I'm one of those weeds. At the end of the day I'm exhausted, my back and legs and hands ache and my face is sunburned. The owner congratulates me on my zeal and presents me with a sack of muri (puffed rice) and fifty rupees in coins. He asks me to come back the next morning at the same time because seeds have to be planted.

I return home accompanied by other children from the neighbouring villages. I can barely carry the sack on my shoulders. It's five o'clock, and I would quite like to go to bed, but I still have to help Ma remove the chaff from the rice grains before cooking them.

The work in the rice paddies is exhausting, but you have to take advantage of it because once the rainy season starts there will be no further work. The owner now pays us a hundred rupees per day. That's double the amount he paid before and as much as all the money that was brought home by everybody's wages. In the evening I carry back the sack of rice clasped to my chest, one hand on top and the other under the packet for fear that it will tear. I cry all the way home. I think that it's the tiredness after so much effort. My mother cooks the rice in a big casserole. I am very hungry and feel dizzy. There are five of us around the dish, and there won't be enough for everyone. I eat sparingly and then retire discreetly. Later in the evening I take Baba's basket and roll some cigarettes. After making hundreds of them I collapse on a straw mattress near the door, fully clothed. I wake up in the middle of the night, freezing cold in the low night temperatures.

Baba is patching the roof so that it won't leak during the monsoon. In the evening when I get home from the rice paddy he asks me if I want to go back to school. I reply that I don't. If I am in the classroom that means that I can't earn money any more in the fields nor roll extra bidis when my father has finished his ten hours of daily work. The maths are simple. It is not profitable to go to school.

Several people came to the village during the day and asked all the families if their children were working, either with them or for an employer. They convinced my father that I ought to go to school. It's obligatory for someone of my age.

'I don't want to go there, and I won't go!'

'Rekha, if you go to school you won't be obliged to go to plant rice shoots for the rest of your life. Look at me! I'm worn out by all these years of labour. I can't sit down any more. I've been inhaling tobacco for such a long time that I have trouble breathing, and my sight is failing.'

'I am going to help you. Josna is away, but I can take your place rolling cigarettes. I know how to do it now. Look, you see that I can easily do five hundred of them. The two of us will make more than a thousand cigarettes a day . . .'

'I don't want to put your future in danger. If you are edu-cated, if you know how to read and write, you will be even more useful to us.'

'You think that's better? Because of the dowry?'

My father is embarrassed by my reply. He looks away and says, 'Yes. Your mother and I hope to pay less if you have some schooling . . .'

'I don't intend to get married.'

'But you'll have to. When you're ten or so we'll find you the best possible husband.'

I must be around seven or eight years old. I can hardly imagine that in less than two years I will be the wife of some man.

'If I go to school it's not to reduce my dowry but to study and to become someone important, someone who earns a good living.'

They came early in the morning. They went from family to family to meet the children one at a time. They asked me what work I was doing and if I was already going to school. I answered that I was happy as I was and that I didn't need to go to school. The people from NCLP were visibly ready for this kind of talk. They told me that my parents were going to be compensated if I was sent to school. There was a Bengali government pro-gramme for this, and the budget had been approved by the executive in New Delhi. From the day that I started going to school regularly my life changed completely.

Saraswati, Budhimuni, Sunita, Afsana – my best friends – and I are in the same school, which is situated a few hundred metres from our houses near the temple of Saraswati, the goddess of knowledge. Our teacher, Atul, is very welcoming. He congratulates us at length for having come and then shows us around the place. Our classroom is on the first floor of a building annexed to the main school. We are a little older, and the teachers are afraid that we won't fit in with the other pupils; besides, our programme is accelerated, the idea being that we will catch up on the basic material in three years, while the other pupils have to study for five years.

We then meet Arjun, our headmaster, who will also be our teacher of mathematics and English. He, too, thanks us for coming and wishes us much success in our new surroundings. He presents each of us with a book, a notebook, a pen, a slate and some pieces of chalk.

The room is big and has two worn-looking blackboards facing one another across the room. There are two big windows covered by grilles, a chair for the teacher and a big rattan mat for the pupils. The class is divided into two. While one half is studying Bengali, the other half is turned towards the second blackboard and learns history or geography. It's very disconcerting because there is no separation, and at times I can't really tell who is speaking and who is teaching what. So I decide to take my place in the front row.

I feel that Atul likes me. He is a good teacher. He is very gentle and never raises his voice. When a pupil doesn't understand a question or has trouble grasping an idea he rephrases his words, while sometimes slipping some clues to the answer into his question. He is a very skilful teacher and always insists that we reply by ourselves, even if it means helping us some-times in quite an obvious way.

The class always begins with the Indian national anthem, and then we launch into some Baul songs – Bengali religious folksongs. Atul compliments me on my voice and tells the other pupils to follow my example. I am flattered but always very shy and embarrassed when I am asked to sing in front of my class-mates. After that we learn Bengali grammar and vocabulary. During these few hours we don't need to work in the rice paddies or anywhere else. Playtime is one of the privileged moments in the day. All that is asked of us is that we play – that we act like children and not adults. We also have classes concerning hygiene and the importance of education in our future lives. So I learn that we ought to wash our hands several times a day and that we should take a shower with soap and shampoo at least once a week.

This first year is by far the most enriching experience I have ever had up to now. I am hard working in class, and I find the lessons easy. What's more I very quickly become one of the best pupils in the class. I know how to count up to a thousand, and I know the alphabet by heart. I understand the importance of what Atul and Arjun are teaching us.

Back home I say that I love school. My mother ignores my enthusiasm and asks me to wash the dishes and tidy the house. I obey out of fear that she will get angry with me. Her glassy eyes seem to bulge from their sockets. It's time to go to see another doctor other than the one in the village – who, as my father says, only prescribes the medicines that he has and not the ones that she needs to get well. Baba is seated on a thick cushion and is mechanically rolling some bidis. He squirms around in all directions to find a comfortable position for his back. I suggest that he go to lie down for a few minutes, and I take the basket and roll some bidis so that he can reach his daily quota.

3
THE EVIL EYE

I have the impression that the screaming is rending the sky and ripping open the moon. How many people are indoors? I don't know. I stopped counting after the fifth or sixth person. In the courtyard of the house the neighbours' children are terrified by my sister's cries. The women weep; the men worry in silence. Some of them think to make themselves useful by praying and invoking the gods. Others tie up their livestock for fear that they will be scared by these terrifying noises and run off into the fields.

'We have to call a doctor,' says one of the villagers.

'At this hour of the night?' replies another.

'What for?' say some others.

'These midwives have come from their village for us. Even though they're from a different community they are childbirth professionals. It's said that they can perform miracles, including when the mother is young or suffering intensely during the contractions,' says a grandmother who has given birth to eight children.

But that night there won't be a miracle. Baba leaves the house with his arms hanging limp by his sides. Everyone looks at the ground, and the embarrassed crowd disperses listlessly. I creep towards the house, and through the half-opened door I can make out my sister Josna surrounded by several women. She is motionless, perhaps already dead. The midwives hold the baby with its head down and pat it harder and harder. There's no reaction from the baby. My mother is slumped sobbing on my sister's chest. I don't know if I ought to enter or go back into the courtyard with the other children. I decide to go back out. This is the second time that my sister has tried unsuccessfully to give birth. Perhaps this time she will even lose her life.

My sister and I are very close in spite of there being nearly ten years between us. We are two partners who like to take care of each other. She looks after me when our parents are away, cooks my meals and takes me to the pond so that I can bathe. Josna is more than a big sister – she is a friend I can confide in, and we share all our secrets without fear.

My parents introduced her to her first husband when she was twelve years old. He was a fellow who came from a neighbouring village, and his parents were farmers. He was neither attractive nor repulsive. He had an ordinary physique with fine down on his upper lip and hardly more hair on top of his head. His big, callused hands convinced my parents that he would be a good husband. His good qualities as a worker, someone capable of founding a family and of feeding it – that was the deciding factor in the eyes of my mother. The meeting took place at our house. His parents came to ask for the hand of Josna, who they had, of course, never seen before. To make a good impression my parents bought a quarter-chicken, a kilo of better quality rice than usual and some rotis spread with oil.

Ma cooked a dish in a sauce. The discussion lasted several hours, and when the moment came to speak in concrete terms about the wedding the two lovebirds were invited to get acquainted.

My sister was embarrassed – and he was, too. They sat on the pavement opposite in plain sight of the two sets of parents. Josna was half turned away, and her veil covered almost all of her head. They spoke, or rather whispered, for several minutes under the amused gaze of the village children.

Later the meal was served, and the men took their places around the table that my father had borrowed from his brother. The women served them the midday meal. The mother of the proposed groom praises the qualities of her son. 'He is a hard worker, young, intelligent. He could have gone to school and become someone important, but somebody had to help cultivate the fields. After all, that's why you have children, isn't it?'

Ma laid out Josna's strong points: her beauty, her youth, her culinary talents and her ability to take care of children. Josna had already been raising her younger brothers and sisters for several years now.

By the time we have *chai* the union is sealed and the dowry fixed at ten thousand rupees. The ceremony will be paid for by the father of the groom. Baba is delighted because he was thinking that he would have to stump up fifteen or twenty thousand rupees and pay half the wedding costs. But it is true that his son-in-law has not been to school nor even been to a town, and so it would be foolish to pay more, especially as he has neither a vehicle, nor personal inheritance, nor rich parents, nor great agricultural lands that could generate comfortable revenues.

The wedding will take place in a month. Everything has been organized during the course of one meal. In around thirty days my older sister will be the responsibility of her future husband and one mouth fewer to feed for Baba. Josna is sad to have to leave the house and to go to live with a man she didn't even know existed this morning and with who she is going to spend the rest of her life.

On the day of the wedding my sister is radiant. Her sari is dotted with sparkling sequins and her hands are decorated with intricate designs in henna. She is swathed in a large piece of white fabric. As for every wedding the whole village is involved. The musicians are Baba's friends, the old carts for the procession belong to the neighbours and the cooking pots that are used to prepare the food for the guests belong to Ma's parents. The rest of the village makes up the wedding procession.

The Hindu priest, facing the couple, celebrates their union and recites their duties for the rest of their lives. The crown of flowers presented to my sister by her husband marks the beginning of singing and dancing that will last for several hours. For reasons of economy the wedding lasts for one day only. Josna's father-in-law can't afford to offer more than that.

During the whole ceremony I saw my sister's fear at the idea of leaving her family. She seemed lost in the middle of all the congratulations, and all those eyes looking at her disturbed her more than they made her happy. We knew each other so well that I didn't have to talk to her to know what she was thinking. She realized that she would never again be a child and that she had just abruptly entered adulthood once and for all – although she was still only an adolescent. I promised to visit her as soon as it was possible. She undertook to come back to see us every month. Her in-laws did not have any objection to that on the condition that Josna didn't stay more than two days and one night.

I couldn't have imagined that after one month of marriage my sister would come back to live with us.

'What's going on?' my father asked when he saw her return, loaded down like a mule.

'He left!'

Ma ran to meet my sister, shook her like a mango tree and asked for explanations. 'What did you do? Why did he leave? And where did he go, anyway?'

'I don't know, Ma. He disappeared two weeks ago. His parents haven't had any news either. They think that he went to join his brother in Calcutta.'

'But you don't just leave your family and your wife on a whim,' my father put in.

'Of course not. She's lying. She must have done something that annoyed him,' Ma shouts.

'I didn't do anything wrong, Ma! I obeyed and did everything they told me to do. I cooked and did the housework without ever turning a hair or protesting . . . and now I'm ruined. Nobody else will ever want me.'

Josna is in tears. The marriage was consummated, she is impure. No other man will want to marry her. Personally I am very happy that she is among us again, but I quickly understand that she will never have a family.

My furious mother, shocked at my sister's return, takes Baba's arm and says, 'Let's go and see the family.'

Ma orders me to go and find her scarf. When I give it to her she strides down the main village street in the direction of the house of Josna's in-laws.

My sister refuses to speak to me. She is curled up on her straw mattress inside the house to escape from the shame. The first neighbours stroll past our house to try to find out more about what's going on. I don't say a word to them.

When the parents return my mother is even more furious than before. My father has a gloomy expression. Not only is their daughter no longer a virgin but the dowry money was wasted even as Baba has gone into debt to pay it.

My mother went to see the *panchayat*, the assembly whose role it is to sort out differences between individuals and villages. She explained the situation to them, but there was nothing to be done. The son disappeared with the money and his parents had no news. They were sincerely sorry about the situation and they knew that their reputation was now sealed and that no one would trust them ever again. Their other sons won't find wives unless they search several dozen kilometres from their village. The local police suggested putting the missing husband and deserter on the list of wanted persons, while explaining that there was almost no chance of finding him if he had taken refuge in a big city like Calcutta. If he had left the state of West Bengal there was no chance of tracing him.

After that Josna cried every day. During a long period of depression she refused to eat. She grew visibly thinner. Every day my mother cursed all the men on earth. She stopped eating, too. Anger and bitterness gnawed away at her.

*

Everything changes when Badhari's father comes to knock on our door and asks to speak to Baba.

'*Namaste*, Karno. I am coming to see you because I hope to find a wife for my son Badhari. Do you know him?'

'No.'

'But you met him at the weekly market. A big, strapping fellow, very fine. He is the biggest of my sons.'

'I don't see very well, but never mind. What makes you say that he could be suitable for my daughter?'

'He was the one who spoke to me about it. He asked for my permission to marry her. I don't have any objection. Even if she has already been married . . .'

'Yes, it's an unhappy experience that the gods put in our path.'

'How much is her dowry?'

'Not very much, I'm afraid. I can offer only ten thousand rupees. But my daughter is still young. She is only twelve and a half years old. What's more, she is beautiful and a good worker. She is employed in a brick factory. She would be a very good catch for anyone who wants to marry her.'

'Then ten thousand rupees it is! It's a deal! He's my last son and I would like to see him start a family before I depart this life.'

It is nothing short of a miracle that has just happened. Ma announces to Josna that she has finally found a husband – a godsend so soon after the first misadventure. My sister, however, remains cautious and is afraid of another unpleasant experience.

A few months after the marriage Josna has some vomiting and dizziness. She is no longer able to go to work at the brick factory. The work is too hard, the fumes too toxic, and she has a constant backache. It's only after a few months that she realizes she is pregnant for the first time.

The childbirth is very painful. The contractions last for several hours. My sister screams for a good part of the day as her mother-in-law looks on, trying to calm her so that she will give birth to her child as quickly as possible. I am worried. I wonder if all women have to suffer the same fate when they give birth. Everyone seems relieved when the first cries of the baby fill the room. The baby is very thin, like his mother. And Josna has no milk. She has to mix a little water and sugar and feed the baby with a teaspoon, although it is too small to open its mouth. It is also too young to have a name. As a precaution and as a superstition parents do not give a definite name to a child until it is a few months old.

The child died a few weeks after its birth.

My sister was devastated. Me, too. I wanted it to live. Baba took care of having the body cremated. None of us was permitted to attend the cremation.

Today my sister gave birth to another baby who lived for only a few hours. The midwives admit to being afraid for Josna's health. They have never seen so many complications during childbirth. They congratulate Josna on having survived the ordeal. My sister goes to the temple of Krishna to thank the god for sparing her life. Badhari makes a donation to the temple so that the avatar of Vishnu may make the coming of their next child easier.

But the gods remained deaf to the young man's requests. The third childbirth was as terrifying as the previous ones. After several hours of pain and cries and tears my sister gave birth to a stillborn baby. Josna seemed unconscious. My mother shook her while shouting prayers and begging the gods to let her keep her daughter. Once again Josna was near death, but she had barely recovered when the problems began again. Badhari's parents judged her unsuitable for motherhood and consequently not worthy to be the wife of their son. They came in person to ask that the couple separate so that their youngest son could marry a fertile woman capable of bearing a child.

'Take your daughter back! We don't want her any more!'

The discussion was heated. The two mothers argued ferociously. The first defended her son's right to have an heir. Ma replied that her daughter was perfectly normal and that she would not let Badhari divorce Josna nor ruin her life and her chances to have a child and start a family. A compromise was achieved after several hours of negotiations: Josna would go to go to see a doctor to find out whether she had a natural malformation preventing her from giving birth properly, the expense payable by Baba to be the equivalent of one week's work. Once the results were known Badhari would have to decide if he wanted to stay with Josna or to separate from her. While they were waiting Josna must return to live at home.

These days are the longest for the family. All my father's money goes for the medical examination. He is up to his neck in debts. Baba doesn't manage to earn enough to buy food. He begs at the doors of the villagers and comes back only with starchy liquid, the water in which the neighbours have boiled their rice.

The doctor's verdict is issued after a few weeks – Josna is perfectly normal. He has detected no malformation. On the

THE STRENGTH TO SAY NO

other hand her age poses a problem: she is too young to give birth. The parents are relieved. Armed with this indisputable diagnosis Baba and Ma go to see Badhari's family and beg them to forget about the divorce. But the young husband considers that he has been patient enough. In spite of his attraction to Josna he must leave her and find another wife. My sister, in one last effort to save her marriage, begs her husband not to abandon her. She implores him to let her have one more chance. Badhari is touched and decides that my sister is after all not at fault, that he should face his destiny rather than blame Josna. He asks his parents to accept her as she is.

But fate won't leave them alone. Although the couple decide not to make a baby right away Josna falls pregnant again. During her whole pregnancy she goes regularly to the temple of Krishna and conserves her strength by staying in bed. She gave up her work in the brick factory. To compensate for the lost income she rolls bidis all day long. The wages are less, but they allow us to buy rice and some vegetables.

At the birth it's a drama again. Josna again has a stillborn baby. Rumours circulate in the village. The neighbours talk about a curse, a bad karma. I take my sister in my arms while she is still covered with sweat. I whisper to her that now she must give up on having a child if she is not to lose her life.

She stays in bed for several days in a tiny room that is also used as a kitchen at the in-laws'. The situation gets complicated. Must she renounce maternity or simply marriage? I am extremely sad for Josna; her face was rounded and beautiful before, but now it looks emaciated.

One wintry morning Josna again prepares to give birth. Sheer madness, according to some of our neighbours, who are convinced that this time she is going to die. My sister is anxious and stressed, but she has to give birth to this child at the risk of losing her life. Her shouts and sobs of pain attract the attention of the entire neighbourhood. After interminable hours of labour Debu is born ('little god' in Hindi). I am in the courtyard, and I pray for him to live for a long time.

4

'LITTLE GOD'

Panicked by the piercing sound of the horn the herd ran off in all directions. The van manoeuvres with great difficulty among this mass of flesh. It tries to force its way through while the shepherd tries to get his animals together again with the help of a stalk of bamboo and incomprehensible sounds. A young calf dashes across just in front of the vehicle to cower against its mother on the other side of the road. The van brakes sharply and the driver shouts at the farmer, but the farmer ignores him as he is busy threatening one of his cows with his staff. Badhari tries to protect himself from the tide of animals whose chaotic behaviour frightens all the villagers gathered at the crossing of the main road and the country road that leads to the hamlet of Sampur.

For some weeks now the men have been returning to the village every evening in a group after several of them were attacked. The thieves take advantage of the half-light of dusk to rob the foolhardy men who risk coming home alone with wages in their pockets along the lane, five kilometres in length, that separates the main road from the house. My brother-in-law has already been robbed at knifepoint. For this reason the villagers now wait for each other in front of the statue of the Hindu god Hanuman set up at the side of the main road, where the public lighting and some traders discourage bandits. The police refuse to intervene in this area after dark, mainly for fear of being the target of attacks by groups of Maoists. This security vacuum has been to the advantage of the bandits, who do not hesitate to abuse the villagers and to relieve the workers of their daily or weekly pay, however small it may be.

The men go alongside the little pond, then beside some fields before starting on the long path that leads to the village. They walk fast; they have to get to the washhouse at the edge of the hamlet of Sampur in less than an hour, before it gets pitch dark. During the trip they exchange the latest news about this or that employer looking for workers for a one-off job. It's also the time to share news about one's family and to hear other people's news.

When he gets home Badhari slips the money he's earned into my sister's hands and puts the plastic shopping bag down on the bed. There are one hundred and fifty rupees, some vegetables and some dry biscuits for Debu.

'We have to take the baby to the temple,' murmurs Badhari, out of breath from the hour of walking as well as a day of labour.

'When?' replies Josna as she puts away the tomatoes and the onions at the foot of the bed, just next to some tin plates and the ashes of the hearth.

'He's going to be almost six months old, and it's time for him to wear a new talisman, a *tabij*.' Josna raises her sari and gives her breast to Debu.

'He's eating better and better, and I have plenty of milk. Everything is going well for the time being, but you're right, I'd be happier if he wore a new *tabij*.'

'Tomorrow he will be even more protected than he is today, and so on for the rest of his life.'

*

Whenever I have the chance I go to stay with Josna and Badhari for a few days. The in-laws don't have any objection to it, and I have learned to make myself useful, especially in helping my sister take care of Debu. My nephew is actually very well protected: he wears a *tabij*, a *kabach* and two *maduri*. The one around his calf carries the blessing of both the moon and the sun – in other words, physical health and internal peace. As for the silk string braided around his waist it allows the body to absorb the nourishment it takes in.

Each of the bracelets on his wrists comes from a scrap merchant in Purulia, but these amulets have undergone a special ritual so that they can act effectively. The bracelet on the upper arm where a little cylinder is attached is meant to keep away the negative waves sent out by wandering souls desperate for nourishment. The *kabach* is used to surmount all the difficulties to come. In case of illness or injury Debu will get well quickly and heal more easily. His destiny will be free of dangerous or fatal events.

Since the birth of Debu his parents have been anxious and fear that he may suffer the same fate as the earlier babies. They follow all the advice that the elders can lavish on them. They go to the temple frequently and fulfil their obligations by making offerings and surrounding their son with lucky charms. If Debu should ever die neither of his parents would ever get over it. The baby who was so wished for is surrounded by affection and by precautions. I look after him with the greatest care – after all, my sister raised me from my earliest days while my parents were working from dawn to dusk in the rice paddies.

*

The time has come to celebrate the ritual of Annaprasan, which marks the moment when babies can take solid food. Josna and Badhari give up the idea of having a party, as is the tradition. They don't have enough money; my brother-in-law's work is barely enough to feed his family. We go to the temple with only the closest relatives: my parents and Badhari's parents, Badhari's his brothers and their children, as well as my brothers and sisters. Other children from the village also join in the ceremony. The Hindu priest recites a *puja* to the gods Krishna and Shiva. He invites the senior males to feed Debu with a ball of rice mixed with milk and sugar. There are several clay pots that contain a pen, a book, metal bracelets and soil. What Debu chooses will determine his future. He plunges his hand into the bracelets. Josna smiles. They symbolize good health and a long life.

Every morning Badhari gets up at dawn and leaves on an empty stomach for Purulia. When he gets to the rickshaw station he has to queue up like a hundred other people.

'Do you have a rickshaw available this morning, Gopal Babu?' my brother-in-law asks the proprietor of an important park for bicycle-taxis.

'I think so, but I won't be able to tell you until about ten o'clock in the morning. I expect some cancellations, but nothing is confirmed at the moment.'

'I'll stick around. I'm counting on you, Gopal Babu. I have to get work – I have a family to feed.'

'Everybody has a family to feed, but I have only a hundred and fifty vehicles. Don't worry, I know that you're honest and you're a good worker. I'm going to find you a place. Don't go away.'

Gopal Babu is an old man with a long white beard that is always carefully trimmed. The whole town of Purulia knows his story. When he was young he got into debt with a local money-lender to buy his own bicycle-taxi so he could go into business for himself. In twenty years Gopal Babu covered tens of thousands of kilometres without ever leaving the town of Purulia or its environs. He never took a day off, not even after the accident with a lorry full of merchandise that cost him the use of one of his arms. The driver of the lorry had driven on without stopping, and some local people found Gopal Babu lying at the side of the road. Ever since then his left arm has been half paralyzed, but the next day Gopal Babu took up his vehicle again and continued to work. He sent his children to school for years. The temptation to employ them was great, but he didn't want one of his sons to suffer what had happened to him. The adolescents grew up and passed their examinations with flying colours and Gopal Babu asked the town authorities to fast-track passports for the boys. Without paying any bribes the old man convinced the communist authorities that they owed him this favour, all the more so because they hadn't done anything at the time of his road accident. That was a clinching argument that the old man had kept up his sleeve to use at the right moment. The boys got their visas and were able to emigrate to the United States. Rather than retire and live off the remittances sent by his children Gopal Babu began to acquire more rickshaws and then hire them out by the day to villagers who didn't have the means to buy a vehicle of their own. As the management of the park became more and more time consuming Gopal Babu stopped driving. At night the rickshaws are kept in the parking area of the depot where two watchmen guard them until early in the morning.

Every day Badhari presents himself at the meeting place in the depot. When there is no rickshaw he waits in front of the stalls, his stomach hollow; he doesn't even have the means to pay for a cup of tea for himself. When a rickshaw becomes free Badhari can breathe again. He knows that he is going to earn some rupees and that the costs of the day are covered. In a few hours he travels several dozen kilometres. Purulia is too small a town to have efficient public transport and too big for people to get around in on foot. A woman asks to go to the market, a man has to get back to his office, children coming out of school have to be taken home. There is no time to lose. Hardly has one customer got off when you have to take on another; the rickshaw should be empty for the shortest amount of time. The interminable negotiations for a few rupees are the most tiresome; sometimes you have to agree to pedal for next to nothing because the competition is fierce.

The rickshaws swarm like flies in this region of Bengal, especially as the Bengalis who have succeeded in crossing the border between Bangladesh and India work for much less. During the day the bikes go all over the place and don't stop except when they have to.

The other danger is a breakdown or a puncture. But Badhari has great initiative: if the chain breaks he pushes the bike to the destination. If the tyre bursts he repairs it in a few minutes, for the hire is expensive. And at the end of the trip half goes to Gopal Babu and half to the driver. At three o'clock Badhari has to stop working because the return trip to the village is long and absolutely must be done in daylight.

For a month my brother-in-law works an average of two days out of three. The rest of the time he waits for things to get better. Gopal Babu suggests that he work at night to earn more money. Badhari could double his wages if he worked until eight or nine o'clock. By leaving midway through the day he is missing the customers who leave their offices at the end of the afternoon, people who go shopping in the evening or quite simply need to get around the town. There have been times when he didn't hesitate to sleep in a corner of the depot, but since the birth of his son he absolutely must return every evening.

For several days I am with the in-laws, and I miss lessons. I have to return to Bararola, especially as I am anxious to get back to school. My sister packs her things – she is going to spend some days at home so that our parents can also enjoy some time with the baby and see how well he is.

At the entrance to the village Josna stops at the temple of Radha. The few metres of concrete seem to be in a state of neglect. No painting has been done; the work isn't going forward very fast. All the villagers are supposed to contribute to the construction of the temple, but no one really has the means to give even a few rupees. The donations are rare, for stomachs are empty. The funding comes mostly from the Mahatos family, the cousins of the great landowners who have made their fortune in the fresh-water fishing industry. In spite of the state of the temple Josna recites some prayers before coming into the courtyard of the house a few minutes later.

Our brothers and sisters mob Debu. They all want to touch

him and play with him. Baba takes the baby in his arms for a few moments before returning him to Josna. He explains that Ma isn't there but out working in the rice paddies. He himself must go and take the bidis to the dealer and get tobacco and leaves for the coming days. I suggest that he take more of it than usual because Josna and I will be able to help him roll bidis whenever we have the chance to do it. Baba tells me that the teachers have come every day to ask for me. I have to return to school as soon as possible.

I got a scolding from Arjun, the head teacher. Arjun didn't even take the time to park his bike in the courtyard. He asks me to explain why I missed the three previous days. I explain that I had to help my sister who had just had a baby. He doesn't want to know about it. Pupils ought to come to school every day except in the case of illness. I promise to stay after school so that my teacher can help me catch up with the lessons I missed.

At the end of the week our teacher tells us about the rights of children. I am surprised to learn that we have rights and that our parents cannot do what they like with us. According to my way of thinking I belong to my procreators and they can do what they want with me until I am married, after which I should abide by the decisions of my future husband. I am fascinated by the idea that we have the right to decide about our lives and that our parents cannot force us to do what they want. If only my sister had been to school she would have had an easier life! Then we go on to a lesson about hygiene in which Atul explains to us that it is important to cut our fingernails regularly. Another discovery! I would never have thought that illnesses could be caused by bacteria on our fingers.

Ma looks after Debu's every need. She is happy to see that this child born in the middle of winter is well and reassured to know that Josna is capable of bearing a child, even if her daughter, with scars all over her abdomen, will have trouble coping with a new pregnancy.

She can't take her eyes off him. 'Fortunately Debu is a boy,' she says.

5

MARRIAGE OFFERS

My father comes into the courtyard with two big plastic sacks. One contains eucalyptus leaves and the other tobacco. He asks me to bring him a bucket of water to soak the leaves. As he puts out his cushion and the tools of his trade I begin the wetting process while telling him what I do in class. I am happy to learn and to discover new things every day. I inform him that dirty fingernails are carriers of disease and that he needs to wash his hands several times a day. He smiles, he who never really knew his mother and has learned everything on the job.

My paternal grandmother, he tells me, died when he was still a child. He remembers her as a woman whose face was marked with pustules who lay for days at a time in a feverish state. She went blind and then the shivers and the hallucinations became more and more frequent. My grandfather had people come who were able to treat her, notably with Ayurvedic methods. It was said that she had to be inoculated with another virus to cure her. I didn't understand what that meant, but that didn't matter because it didn't work. She died a few days later in terrible suffering. My grandfather never wanted to marry again, so Baba was brought up by his father's family: his uncles and aunts and his grandmother. He went to school for only a few years. He knows how to count but not to read. When something has to be written he copies out the characters from memory – most of the time without making the connection between the letters. As his family owned no land they all worked as agricultural labourers. Around the age of ten Baba learned to roll bidis, and since then that has been his main activity.

The members of our caste marry around the age of ten. I was nine when my parents suggested finding me a husband. I was furious with my mother who talked about it first and enraged with my father who wasn't opposed to the idea. My parents wanted me to find a husband just then because my dowry was the best it could be – more than ten thousand rupees! I protested vigorously about this plan and ran to take refuge at my uncle's a few doors away. My parents came to get me, but I was so angry that I refused to see them and even to sleep at home that night. I was terrified at the idea of having the same experience as my older sister. My uncle agreed that I could spend the night at his house, as I had often done before. He reassured my parents and promised to bring me home the next day. My uncle didn't ask me what we were quarrelling about. I went home the next day. I was convinced that, considering my reaction, my parents would have given up their idea. But for fear of a new confrontation I left immediately for school.

Our teacher teaches us history, English, mathematics and Bengali literature. I am always chosen to sing the national anthem or the prayers. In spite of my mediocre voice the head teacher insists that I be the one who leads the other pupils. I try hard to make sounds come out of my throat, to keep my mind on the words in spite of the fear that is stifling me.

As always on the last day of the week we get to have a half-day of discussion, in the course of which our teachers inform us about things other than our school subjects. This week it's not about hygiene but about scientific experiments at the museum of natural sciences in Purulia. I don't really like this place – except perhaps the workshop where you have to make mixtures of liquids and identify the smells – but the advantage of these outings is that we are with all the other pupils of the school, and that allows us to meet children who began school at the normal age. Pinky is one of those. She is shy and very reserved; she is slim, her hair is almost blonde and she has big, bright eyes. Her parents are as poor as the other inhabitants of the village. Her father went away several years ago – first to Purulia, where he became a bus driver, and then to Calcutta, where he claimed to have a taxi. For years Pinky's mother regularly received money through intermediaries that the father found in town. He was contacted by an agency that specialized in placements abroad. He left India for a country in the Middle East where he was supposedly recruited as a private chauffeur. After a few months the mother received no further money nor even any news of her husband. The telephone rings without being answered regardless of the time that Pinky's mother calls.

From then on she raised Pinky and her other children by herself. She works with my sister in the brick factory. All day long the women dig clay with their bare hands and make bricks using a mould marked with the name of the owner, going back and forth over several hundred metres to dry them in the sun. Pinky and I first struck up a friendship during these school outings. She knows a lot of things, but her reserved manner makes her seem rather stand-offish. She doesn't have many friends, and very few children like to play with her. During playtime she stays by herself in a corner of the yard.

Arjun, the head teacher, calls us together and asks us to be sure to be at school the next week. I expect another school outing to the museum.

When I get back home the subject of marriage is the centre of the conversation again. The son of one of my uncles has asked to marry me. Ma tries to convince me to meet him.

'He's a relative and is ready to accept the dowry that we're offering.'

'I don't care where he comes from and what he's ready to accept. I don't want to get married, and that's final!'

'Don't be selfish. Think of your family. You think that your father can keep on working in these conditions? His back hurts constantly and he has trouble breathing because of inhaling tobacco for years, and he does all that to feed you. Do you realize the sacrifices that he has been making all this time?'

'I'll help him. I'm quite willing to work after school so that he can make his daily quota of cigarettes.'

'You understand nothing, my girl. You cost us too much, and if we don't get you married while you are young and attractive nobody else will want you.'

'I don't want to get married, do you hear me? I am enrolled at the school, and I intend to keep going there!'

'You're not the one who decides! The Kalindis all marry at your age. If you want to keep on studying you can sort that out with your husband. Our duty as parents is to find you a husband before it's too late.'

'I don't want to get married!'

The conversation breaks down into yelling. My father interrupts us: 'Stop carrying on like that, both of you! Do you want the whole village to hear you?'

'Your daughter is stubborn and doesn't understand her luck in having so many marriage offers. She's only thinking of herself and her blasted school. As if food was free! I told you that enrolment at the school was a bad idea, but you didn't listen to me. This is the result. You can deal with it. And then you can go and explain to your nephew that he can't marry your daughter Rekha, because according to the latest news she's the one who decides not you!'

'Be reasonable, Rekha, this marriage offer is a chance for you. You ought to seize it, both for your own good and also for the good of your family. Think of your brothers and sisters, please,' whispers my father in an affectionate tone.

'I don't care! I want to go on learning and working at my studies. That's what you advised me to do not so long ago. Remember?'

'Yes, but that was temporary. We sent you to school while we were waiting for you to find a husband. Now you don't need to study any more.'

'Temporary? But you know how difficult school is! I am one of the best in the class, and you want me to abandon everything just because a boy who doesn't even know me wants a wife in his house?'

'When I married your mother I didn't know her either. That didn't prevent us from starting a family . . .'

'A family that you have trouble feeding! Is that the kind of future you want for your children?'

THE STRENGTH TO SAY NO

I went off in the direction of my uncle's house, taking the maze of paths among the dried-mud houses to cover my tracks. I pushed the little metal door, praying that it wouldn't squeak as it usually did. I climbed the half-built stairs while avoiding meeting my uncle's in-laws. I settled down on the big concrete terrace where I couldn't be seen. From above I gazed at the well outside the house. One after the other the women went there to draw buckets of water. Some children filled used oil cans. In the distance the workers were digging in their fields. I envied the young boy who was digging near his father. He at least seemed to be master of his own destiny. Down below I saw my uncle's mother-in-law. Her arms looked like chicken legs. She had only a thin layer of flesh on her bones, but in spite of that she worked the earth of the garden to plant some tomatoes. Since she was a widow she lived with my uncle, and to thank him for his hospitality she makes herself useful all day long. My uncle seized an incredible opportunity when he bought a large plot of land adjoining his house. In theory the well belongs to him, but he lets the villagers use it so that they won't have to walk several kilometres to get water. His generosity is very much appreciated in Bararola.

I hid away on the terrace as the sun went down. I wondered how long I would have to reject the marriage offers that were pouring in. I went to sleep, but my uncle woke me up to suggest coming to the room downstairs. For fear that I would fall over the side he helped me get down the stairs without a guardrail.

The next day I went straight to school without going to our house. It was out of the question to meet my mother, who I imagined must be furious with me. When I got home after school a boy accompanied by his parents was in the house. My mother introduced them to me. I understood what was being plotted and when they asked me what I thought of the young man I didn't answer.

'Are you sure she agrees?' asked the boy's mother.

'Yes, yes!' replied my mother. 'She is shy and reserved, but we spoke to her yesterday. She knows what she ought to do . . .'

I hid out in a corner of the yard, my legs doubled up against my stomach.

'And how old is she?' the mother asked.

'She's coming up for ten. She is very gifted, you know. We've sent her to school so that she will be educated, and she's top of the class. Her teachers are very proud of her. They say that she is much more intelligent than the other pupils.'

'Ah! Very good! Nowadays children should go to school. It's very useful . . .'

I wonder how this woman can know what is said or done in a school – especially as I suspect that her son has never set foot in one.

'I don't know how to cook, and I don't like children,' I say in a cold and determined tone.

'Oh yes?' replies the mother sharply. 'But you are going to learn, I'm sure of it . . .'

'I don't think so. I eat very little, and neither my older sister nor my mother has taught me.'

'She exaggerates. She lacks confidence in herself,' my mother says, trying to reassure the other woman. 'She has taken care of her brothers and sisters since she was quite small . . . I know what she's worth. She's very gifted.'

'Yes, she seems gifted, but my problem is that she's too dark

. . . You see? Compared with my son, who is lighter . . . How much is the dowry? I mean, bearing in mind this difference in skin colour?'

I continued to listen to this discussion – or, rather, negotiation, I should say – that was all about me. I felt that Ma wanted a firm commitment on their part. That's enough. I couldn't bear this masquerade any longer. I got up and headed for the young man, who must have been be five or six years older than I.

'You know the story of Kishalaya?'

'No. What is it?'

'He's a brahmin who frees a tiger from its cage and makes it promise not to eat him in exchange for its freedom. It's a traditional tale of Bengal, but never mind. You know how to sing Baul?'

'No.'

'I am always chosen to perform the Indian national anthem and the traditional songs of Bengal. Do you know that most children's diseases are spread by mosquito bites?'

'No, I didn't know that.'

'I learned all that at school, just as I learned the importance of hygiene, reading and mathematics, and I can't see myself abandoning all that to marry you!'

With that I turned on my heel and went back into the room where the parents were still arguing about the wedding and the dowry.

'Your son is an idiot! I won't marry him whatever my parents say!'

I knew that my parents were going to be embarrassed and get a bad reputation, but I couldn't see any other way to get me out of this trap. The family went away. My mother gave me a furious look, and my father took the villagers back home, all the time offering profuse apologies.

As soon as I enter the gate of the school I feel a sense of liberation. I know that here I am protected by my teachers. They are the ones who taught us that in spite of our ages we can refuse to go along with our parents' plans. I feel like asking for advice from Atul, the teacher, but I decide against it, thinking that my parents have understood the lesson and that it's not worth embarrassing them any more by letting the incident reach the ears of the teachers. Arjun drops in on the class to remind us that everyone should be present next Friday and that no one should leave the class before he has finished his talk. We try to find out what he is going to say to us, but he won't say a word. He simply states that it's important and that he wants to see all of us on that day.

After the class I had no wish to go back home, where remonstrations very probably awaited me. I went off to Afsana's and we played the tag game of *kho kho* until my little brother came to get me.

The telephone rings inside the house, and Ma hands it to me. it's my cousin Sathya, the daughter of my paternal aunt, and she wants to speak to me. She is about the same age as my big sister, and we understand each other particularly well. I've sometimes spent several days at my aunt's in her little hamlet, which is an hour from us by bus. The whole family makes rattan furniture, and the men then sell it at the market. Sathya tells me that her cousin would very much like to come with his parents to meet me. I am astonished by this request. If she wants to come to pay us a visit, she knows very well that she's welcome.

'Why are you talking to me about your cousin?'

'He would like to marry you. We've learned that your parents want you to marry, and he is interested.'

I reply that she must have misunderstood because I do not intend to get married. It's not worth the trip because my answer will be identical even if he is standing in front of me. I will not change my mind. I ring off and hand the telephone back to my mother. I don't say a word. She has obviously heard everything.

I understood that my parents had the firm intention of getting me married, most likely before the next winter. Ma is too busy nursing my brother Tapan to work in the rice paddies any more. Baba no longer manages to earn enough money. The price of food is going up, and we have to drink the water that rice was boiled in. It is becoming more and more difficult to go on like this. Are my parents right? Must I ease out of the family environment and leave room for my younger brothers and sisters? I feel guilty that I was ever born.

On Friday Arjun drops in on each of the classes. He asks the teachers if anyone is missing. Some pupils are absent; but not to worry – Arjun gets on his bike and visits each of the families with a truant child.

We are repeating words in English that Atul has written on the blackboard. With the help of a pointer he indicates the verbs that we have to say out loud. The lesson is finished. Atul asks us to stay quietly seated while he goes to get the headmaster.

Arjun thanks us for being there and tells us that we are

advancing spectacularly and that we must persist in our efforts so that we will have a good enough standard when we join the upper classes. He is smiling and less abrupt than when he teaches our class.

'Do you know what you ought to do once a day?' Arjun asks the class at large.

'Wash our hands!' we all chorus.

'Very good. And what should you do at least once a week?'

'Cut our fingernails!'

'Very good. Today I am going to talk to you about pregnant girls. Do you know what "pregnant" means?'

'That means that the girl is going to have a baby,' replies Budhimuni, one of my ex-friends. I've been angry with her these last few weeks.

'Very good. Do you know how to tell if someone is pregnant?'

Silence. Nobody knows. Arjun rephrases the question. 'Do you know what the symptoms of pregnancy are?'

'You have a fever and you throw up.'

'Very good, Rekha. Any other symptoms?'

'The breasts get bigger because there is milk in them and the belly gets bigger as the baby grows.'

'That's right.'

'The childbirth is very painful and sometimes it happens that the baby is born dead. Or it lives for only a few weeks because it is very weak. Making a baby doesn't work every time. That's why couples begin again. Sometimes the mother can lose her life while giving life.'

'That's right again, Rekha,' says Arjun, visibly surprised that I know so much about the subject. 'But if the pregnancies are difficult it is also because the mothers are too young to give birth to a child. That is the subject of this discussion. A woman can have as many children as she wants on the condition that her body is ready. If she is too young, she can die.'

Other pupils speak up and ask questions. I know most of the answers since I've seen my older sister's unfortunate pregnancies. At the end of the lesson Arjun thanks us for attending this educational discussion. We put our things away and say goodbye to our teachers. I am going towards the exit when Arjun asks me to stay behind for a few minutes.

Rekha Kalindi was eleven years old when the former Indian
president, Pratibha Singh Patil, told her, 'I am hopeful and
sure that you will be an inspiration to other young girls. So
that our country can eliminate this notion of marriage
between two children at the cost of their education, their
future and ultimately their happiness.'

Rekha helps her father (below, watched by his youngest child), who has been rolling traditional Indian cigarettes (bidis) for decades. The low wage is barely enough to feed the whole family.

A young Bengali girl carrying wood in Rekha's village of
Bararola

'Despite legislations and some efforts by government and
non-government agencies to educate the people about the
dangers of early marriage, prejudices and beliefs underlying
the preference continue in India. In West Bengal, too, there
is a silent complicity to child marriage; many rural
communities treat it as normal and routine.' – Extract from
'Child Marriage in Rural West Bengal: Status and
Challenges', Biswajit Ghosh and Ananda Mohan Kar,
Indian Journal of Development Research and Social Action

Left: Rekha's mother was at first not supportive of Rekha and beat and starved her daughter when she refused to marry.

Below: Rekha cycling through her home village of Bararola as young men and boys play football

Right: Rekha's father occasionally plays drums in religious festivals and political marches to earn a little more money to support his family.

Below: Rekha and all her family in Bararola village

Rekha's teacher, Atul, has been a key character in her life. He not only supported her when she refused to marry but encouraged her to continue to attend school so that she could have a better education and a better life.

Josna, Rekha's older sister, suffered greatly when she became a mother at just twelve years old. This strongly influenced Rekha's determination to defy her parents' wishes for her to be married off at eleven.

Rekha and her mother

Rekha at the door of her sister Josna's home

Rekha visiting a school to speak her of experiences and how children facing the same situation should question tradition and expectations

After Rekha's speech in front of the children their teacher congratulates her for her bold choice in refusing early marriage.

6

SPEECH

No pupil has ever entered this room before. The double doors are fastened by a latch and two big padlocks. Arjun looks among his big bunch of keys for the right one. He slips off his sandals with an automatic movement, and I do the same. The concrete floor is cool. A few shafts of sunlight penetrate through a little window covered by a screen with flaking paint. A bulb is suspended from the ceiling by a long cord that comes down almost to the level of a little wooden table. A fan moves the air.

The headmaster looks serious. He pushes a few sheets of paper to the side of the desk and sits down on the plastic chair. I remain standing, my eyes lowered, waiting for Arjun to speak to me. He is very strict, and all the pupils are afraid of him, especially me. He takes his mobile phone out of his pocket and switches it off. I wait for punishment or a serious telling-off about my behaviour towards Saraswati – I had a fight with her a few days ago. I know in advance that he will pay no attention to my arguments and that he'll never understand that she has turned my friends against me.

'Where did you learn all that?'

'What?'

'Those symptoms of pregnancy, the side-effects?' he asks me in an unusual tone of voice, both gentle and warm.

'I noticed it by myself.'

'Have you already been pregnant?'

'No, sir, it wasn't me I was talking about but my big sister.'

'What happened to her?'

'She threw up a lot. I thought she was ill, and when I asked my parents to take her to the doctor they said that it was normal . . .'

'She was pregnant?'

'Yes, but at the time I didn't know that. Her belly wasn't round – it was just like usual.'

'And then?'

'Her pains became more and more frequent. She didn't eat normally, she was in a bad mood, she often complained, sometimes even about me although we have always been very close. At night she hardly slept at all. I would see her pacing around in the yard or in the room. The owner of the brick factory called her back because there was a lot of business, but she didn't want to go because the work conditions and the life there were very difficult. The workers slept in sheet-metal huts without water and without electricity. My mother urged her to accept because the pay was significant and could turn out to be crucial in the coming months. I didn't understand at that time what she meant, but now I know that she was talking about the future birth.'

'Sit down, Rekha,' Arjun says softly, placing a wooden chair in front of his desk.

I sat down while keeping my schoolbag hugged to my chest. I would never have thought that the headmaster of my school, under his authoritarian and brusque demeanour, was capable of listening to and showing kindness to his pupils.

'She went there – she took the bus that goes along the

national road. My mother prepared two hard-boiled eggs for her and a little rice in a plastic bag. For several weeks we received no further news of her, but that was the way it always was when she went to the factory. In the middle of the day the owner phoned and asked to speak to my parents. My mother cried while Baba's face became more and more blank. He put down his cigarettes and his tobacco basket and took the phone from my mother's hands. I heard him say that he would come to get his daughter at once. Late in the evening when they came home, my sister was pale, feverish and her belly had swollen up. She didn't say anything. My mother took her in her arms before carefully laying her down inside the house. She reassured me and told me that my sister was pregnant and that her condition was normal. I didn't have to be worried.'

'What happened to her?' asked the headmaster, hanging on my words.

'She had fainted. The workers brought her round by throwing buckets of water on her face. The boss panicked – he thought that she was dead and imagined himself already accused of causing her death. He gave her the equivalent of a month's wages in cash on the condition that she cleared off.'

'Did you see a doctor?'

'I asked my parents to send her to a doctor. I was convinced that my sister was dying and was going to go any minute. Her eyes were glassy and she was trembling. She seemed out like a candle when you've blown on the wick. I had never seen her like that. She is always smiling, always in a good mood; we have always understood each other very well. This time I had the impression that she didn't even recognize me, that I was just another stranger among others. The village doctor came to see her late in the afternoon. He just recommended she rest and not do anything but stay in bed all day. Her belly became rounder as time went on. In spite of her pains she was delivered of a little boy.' I decide to leave out the miscarriages and the deaths of the babies she'd had before that one.

'This labour went all right?'

'Yes, sir. It lasted for a long time. It was in the winter, and it was cold. There were a lot of people with my sister trying to sooth her during the pains, and she gave birth to a fine little boy. She is very well now.'

'And the baby is well, too?'

'Yes, sir. We were very afraid that he wouldn't make it, but it was OK. He is fine, and he's been eating solid food for a little while now.'

'And you? Your parents take good care of you? Have they tried to marry you off, for example?'

'No, no one has ever forced me to do anything at all. Everything is fine. I help my mother with the housework, and when I can I give my father a hand so that he can make more cigarettes. He is paid according to the number he makes, you know.'

I don't want to tell him about the different marriage offers.

'Very good. Thank you, Rekha. You can go now,' Arjun says, getting absorbed in his papers.

I didn't dare believe that he hadn't mentioned the quarrel with Saraswati! She had really annoyed me by telling all my friends that if I didn't want to be married it was because I had a boyfriend I was seeing on the sly. It's obviously false, but all the kids in the village have fallen for it. In spite of my denials I am seen by certain people as a girl without virtue.

Budhimuni, my neighbour and friend from infancy who understood the reason for my refusal, advised me not to give in to my parents' propositions. That was mainly because if I had agreed and consequently had to give up school she would have been obliged to quit, too.

Whatever her motives, Budhimuni takes my side while that pest Saraswati spreads false rumours. I had no other choice than to slap her in front of everybody to show that I disapprove of this kind of talk that tarnishes not only my reputation but also that of my parents. If I had done nothing I would have been shunned immediately, and my family might have believed her lies. Atul separated us, but if Arjun didn't refer to it it must be because my teacher didn't tell him about it. His support encourages me to work still harder and be the best pupil in the class. I must get into the regular class as soon as possible.

Baba has cramps in his hands. He can't move his fingers any more. I put away my exercise books and I grab the tobacco basket. I roll a few hundred cigarettes. That isn't enough, and we are far from the thousand bidis per day that we have to do. My mother prepares a little rice with curry powder for dinner, which is the only real meal of the day. The next morning for breakfast we drink the water the rice was boiled in. It is bitter because Ma left it on the fire for too long the day before. I leave for school, my stomach rumbling from the effect of that foul drink.

*

At the end of the morning we receive a visit from the deputy minister of labour of the state of Bengal. Atul told us about it a few minutes beforehand. He is an important person, and we must make the best possible impression both of ourselves and of the school. Those people help us every day by defending our rights in public institutions. I feel a little weak, and I'm dizzy. I have eaten nothing solid since a few balls of rice last evening.

Mr Kundu looks like a politician. He has hardly any hair on top of his head – just one long strand remains, which he carefully replaces when it falls over his face. He is very informal, and in a few minutes he has broken the ice with his stories, which reveal that he, too, began school late. He was proof that a person could succeed in spite of an education that was outside the conventional pattern.

'I come from a distant region but one where the customs are similar to the ones here. I had to interrupt my schooling to go to work. Fortunately, because I am a boy my parents let me make my own decisions. For some years I combined school and work. And I have to tell you that you, too, you never have to sacrifice your education for paid work.'

'But what about when our parents don't earn enough?' I asked, calling out my question in a clumsy way, too direct and not respectful enough. The pupils turn around to look at me. The headmaster, a bit embarrassed, tries to make up for my clumsiness.

'Rekha, stand up and ask the question that you want to ask Mr Kundu. I am sure that he can provide you with an answer, isn't that right, sir?'

'She's right! The problem is that the parents don't earn

enough, and that has consequences for your lives. They need to decide what they really want: to have you earn a few rupees so that the family is better off now or to invest in your future so that your children won't have to make this kind of choice? I am happy that you've raised this point. What's your name again?'

'Rekha. Rekha Kalindi, sir. I am the daughter of Karno Kalindi, who rolls cigarettes all day long, but that's not enough to feed us all.'

'Rekha, in our programme we essentially target poor families because they are in economic distress that forces them to make their children go out to work. But this is not the right solution; it's a short-term vision and Mr Arjun's teaching team is here to help you.'

'What should we tell them when they ask us to stop going to school?'

'You should tell them in the first instance that you do not agree. Haven't your teachers taught you that you have rights, one of which is that you can say no to your parents when they suggest that you abandon your schooling?'

'Yessss!' the whole room choruses.

'Very good. You should also remind them that school is mandatory and that to give it up is not an option. If your parents insist you absolutely must talk about it with Atul and Arjun. They can help you, and it's up to them to intervene when such a situation arises.'

I ask, 'But isn't it self-centred to put our future first? Shouldn't we help our parents?'

'That's not wrong, but it's not entirely right, either. The Indian government is behind you. The president, the president of Congress and the prime minister are working so that you'll no longer be faced with this kind of dilemma. You owe respect and obedience to your parents, but only when it's to do with your personal education in the context of the family. I repeat,: school is obligatory for all children – that's what our government says. The prime minister has reiterated it time and again. I know very well that all this seems abstract to you, but it's very real, and your teachers are there for you. I have also come to tell you that we're going to organize a major show at the museum of natural sciences in Purulia. I need two pupils to give a speech about school, what it means to you and whether you think that your life is better since you've been enrolled in it. Who wants to do it?'

Nobody speaks up. People look at Arjun and Atul, as if it were up to them to decide.

'I would like to speak as long as I don't have to sing,' I say.

'Everybody has to sing a song, as well as the national anthem. That's not so hard, is it?'

'If everybody sings, then I'm happy to sing, but I don't want to be the only one.'

'Fine! One other volunteer, a boy for balance?' says Mr Kundu, replacing the strand of hair on his head.

Once more, no one comes forward. Arjun suggests Rajat, the other good pupil of the class. I would have liked Pinky to volunteer. She is undoubtedly the poorest among us, with an absent father, and would be in a good position to explain why she continues to go to school while her family survives only thanks to the help of her uncle.

Back at home my mother is still furious with me. I hurry straight to my father and offer to help him. He has been in a rush these past few days because he hasn't rolled enough cigarettes. The dealer is impatient because he can't manage to fill his orders. He threatens to reduce Baba's quota. The two of us go faster. The hand movements have become so automatic that I even have time to tell him about the visit of the deputy minister and that I am going to make a speech in front of the other children of the region at the museum of natural sciences. He is proud of me and says not to worry about my future. I know that in his mind that means that my dowry will be less important the more educated I am, but I'm relieved at his words. I double my speed, and some hours later Baba takes the bidis to the wholesaler.

He comes back with a new load of tobacco, some leaves and strings and some banknotes in his pocket. On his way home he stopped at the little local market where he bought some rice, some wheat, a small container of oil and some vegetables. There have been times during these last few days when we had nothing but rice water for a meal. Ma puts the rice into a cooking pot before filling it with water. The *panta bhat* – a dish of left-over rice – keeps for a long time, resists the heat and is said to have properties to withstand high temperatures. The cooking water is always carefully saved.

My mother weaves bamboo baskets – as did the first inhabitants of Bararola. It is not very profitable, but it gives us a supplementary income and something to buy eggs with, especially for the youngest children. My big brother, Dipak, makes trips into town to find a job that pays more than working in the rice paddies.

*

We climb on to the bus for Purulia. The teachers warn us that no one is to get off before we reach the terminus. They hand the tickets subsidized by the State of Bengal to the driver, who mutters about this army of children that he doesn't get much for even though they fill the whole bus. In Purulia we walk a few hundred metres past dozens of stalls with appetizing dishes arranged in a geometric form.

Inside the museum there are several hundred of us. Most are pupils of the region and all are taking part in the cultural programme. In all, ninety schools are gathered together. Some have prepared performances of traditional dance, others are organizing reading or theatre workshops. One of the groups has come accompanied by a . . . python! It has to be measured with a measuring tape. I keep my distance from this animal that frightens me as much as it attracts me. My classmate Ashok is thrilled to bits. He throws himself on the reptile and strokes it as though it were an affectionate kitten. It is 1.95 metres long; the teachers ask us to convert the measurement into yards. Further away you have to smell some spices and foods in identical pots without labels. I am more comfortable with conversions of measurements than with smells.

Mr Kundu is there; he goes from workshop to workshop, joking with the pupils, encouraging those who are struggling to read the inscriptions in English and introducing the pupils to each other.

At the end of the morning we are all called into the big conference room. The deputy minister of labour announces the programme: there will be songs, dances and speeches. I'm scared to death at the idea of getting up on the platform and speaking in front of so many people. The first pupil climbs up, introduces himself and then launches into a poem in Bengali. The applause is richly deserved. Then my turn comes. I have a lump in my throat from stage fright. Mr Kundu says some encouraging words to me. I recite the verse perfectly. My voice is clear, the pupils applaud and I run back to my seat. My teacher congratulates me discreetly.

A few minutes later Mr Kundu asks me to come to speak at the rostrum. In front of the microphone my fear disappears. I introduce myself and say what I did before I enrolled in school. I talked about everything in detail – the work in the rice paddies, how I learned to roll bidis in order to help my father, that the plan was for me to go to the brick factory like my sister and her husband's family. I also told them how I was happy at school, that the work there was not only easier but also more fruitful, because I feel sure that with the knowledge that I acquire there I will be able to earn more money than the rest of my family and give them a better life in the future.

I am getting carried away, and I begin to describe the proposals of marriage that my parents made to me as well as my refusal to obey. Am I right not to listen to my parents? I reply before anyone can interrupt me. Yes, because they do not realize that they are putting my future at risk. Am I against marriage? No, but it is too early for me to get married to anybody, no matter who he is. I have witnessed the distress of my sister, who didn't even know that she was pregnant only a few months after her arranged marriage. I saw her give painful birth to four babies who all died. I didn't want to go through all that myself. I say what I have felt all during these last years, motivated by the feeling that I am right to refuse my parents' offers. I have no idea how much time has passed since the beginning of my talk.

Half an hour, perhaps an hour? Every time I tackle a point, a new idea comes to mind.

At the end of my speech, the pupils applaud warmly for many minutes. I blush and I am staggered by their reaction. I go back to my place, but the kids get up and come to shake my hand; the girls give me a hug. I would never have thought that they would agree with me. I was expecting to be booed and treated like a bad girl. Mr Kundu tries to clear some space around me. He asks the kids to go back to their seats. He goes up on the platform, replaces the strand of hair and congratulates me at length for this speech.

'What Rekha Kalindi is going through many of you are also experiencing. When a situation like this arises you should not hesitate to talk about it with your teachers. They have answers and can help you.'

After the speech a dozen journalists come up to see me. They ask me for further details about my story; they ask if what I said really happened as I described it. Several cameras are placed in a semicircle around me. The microphones are held out in my direction, and I repeat what I said on the stage. Arjun, Atul and Mr Kundu come one by one to congratulate me. The deputy minister tells me that we are going to see each other again very soon. I think of my parents' reaction when they find out that I have put our lives on display in front of all these people . . .

I go back into the house quietly and go to the courtyard to be by myself, alone with my exercise books. Ma snatches the slate from my hands and orders me to go fetch some wood to use in preparing the meal. I comply with her orders without arguing. That doesn't do any good when she's in this state.

'I'm on to your game, you little hussy!'

'What game? What are you talking about?'

'I've heard what the kids in the village are saying about you. In front of us you refuse our marriage offers, but behind our backs you go with boys!'

'I don't go with anybody! Who told you that? You shouldn't believe those brats!'

'Oh no? And why should I believe you? Because you're so sincere and perfectly behaved, perhaps? I'm going to speak to your father, and you'll marry the boy who's chosen for you, whether you like it or not!'

'I'm not marrying anybody. Leave me alone, you old witch!'

The words are hardly out of my mouth when my cheek is red from the slap. My mother takes me by the hair and continues to hit me. I try to get away, but she holds me tight with one hand while the other grabs a stick. I cry and I shout, but nobody comes to intervene. After several minutes she stops. I remain lying on the floor, shaking from fear that she might start hitting me again.

7

PRESSURE

The wind was dry and cold. I heard the village children in the distance playing with a ball or trying to ride bicycles. Their carefree attitude contrasted with my state of mind. I daubed a little water on my bruises, but that didn't make any difference to the pain. I rummaged in Baba's things and found a little pot of camphor cream. I gathered my scattered exercise books and sat huddled up in a corner of the room. My finger followed the letters, and I read in silence for fear that I would be discovered.

My big brother Dipak came home sooner than expected. Since he stopped going to school, he has been running a little cardamom-tea shop not far from the statue of Hanuman beside the national road. He understands immediately that I have been hit.

'Ma?'

I nod without saying anything. He puts down his two big kettles and the rest of his equipment before leaving the room, annoyed at not being in a position to reason with our parents about my projected marriage.

At the market one of Baba's friends called to him and held out a newspaper.

'This is your daughter, isn't it?'

'Yes, that's Rekha. What's she doing in the paper?'

'How should I know? But look, she's also in this paper and in this one, too.'

'What's it all about?' Baba asked.

'I haven't the least idea. Just because I sell papers doesn't mean I read them!' says the merchant with a smile of complicity to his neighbour, standing between a mound of garlic and another one of red peppers.

'But you know how to read, don't you? Can you tell me what is written in this article under the photo?'

'Give me five rupees first. If all my customers were like you, I'd spend my time reciting the information from these newspapers and go home in the evening without a penny in my pocket.' He replied with the same mischievous tone, but turning this time to his neighbour on the left who feigned a friendly smile.

'Here you are,' my father said, giving him the money. 'Tell me what's in the paper now!'

The merchant took a pair of half-moon glasses out of his shirt pocket after throwing the coins into a box on the floor near a plastic sheet where magazines were displayed. He murmured for a few seconds while Baba fidgeted impatiently.

'They say that this girl set off thunderous applause at the museum in Purulia when she made a speech that was incredible for her age . . .'

'What did she say?'

'Wait, I'm reading the rest of it,' said the merchant as he continued to murmur to himself. 'She says that her sister had several miscarriages because she was too young to have a child when she fell pregnant . . . It also says that her parents want to marry her off without her consent before next winter. She tries to refuse, her parents insist on the wedding taking place, mainly because they don't want to feed her any more . . . Who does she think she is, this kid, talking about this kind of thing in public? If I were her father I would have given her a good thrashing long before this! That's quite right, don't you agree?'

Baba grabbed the paper out of his hands and rushed home. On his way, several people stopped him and asked if it was really his daughter they had seen yesterday on television. Baba couldn't believe his eyes or his ears. Rekha had gone around talking about everything that happened in the family circle to the newspapers and on television channels. In no time they will be the laughing stock of the whole village, the whole region and perhaps even of all of Bengal. Ma was going to be furious.

Kitchen utensils fly in my direction. Insults rain down. I get a ladle, some spoons and even the cooking pot. I try to protect myself by curling up into a ball, but my mother takes me by the hair and knocks me down. I yell, I cry, I beg her to stop hitting me. Baba holds her back, and my brother Dipak helps me up. He orders me to hide out at my uncle's and not to move from there before he comes to get me. In the courtyard I spot a newspaper with a big picture of me. I realize that my words at the museum in Purulia have brought on my mother's wrath.

I hear her yell at my father, 'You see what your daughter is capable of? She's humiliating us in front of the whole village, that little hussy!'

Baba tries to calm her down by saying that the damage is done, that now they have to think about what to do and say in their defence, especially as the authorities, the school and the *panchayat* might interfere. This is bound to be only the beginning of their problems.

It got too dangerous to listen to the rest of the conversation at the door. My mother was capable of wringing my neck in a fit of anger. I reassured my brothers and sisters, who were disturbed by the violence of the scene and the behaviour of our mother. She seemed to be possessed by demons. I took refuge, as my brother suggested, with my father's family. On the terrace I spelled out the newspaper article. It mentioned everything: the miscarriages, the proposals of marriage, the conditions of life at home and so on. I understood why Ma flew off the handle. The journalists didn't spare any detail. My older brother confirmed my fears.

'Why did you do that, Rekha? It's insane. Ma is beside herself. She's furious with you.'

'I just told the truth, nothing more.'

'In the newspapers. On the telly. On the radio. You realize that everybody is going to know all this stuff? What are people going to think of us?'

'I don't care!'

'You can't say that. The whole family is going to be – and already is – the laughing stock of everybody. The situation can spin out of control very quickly, to say nothing of the problems this can cause.'

'I said, and repeated several times, to our parents that I didn't want to be married, but they didn't even try to listen to me. They spent their time introducing me to suitors. However much I refuse them they just keep banging on about it. They threatened me for weeks. You see how they are. You, too, you were right about it, you know very well how it happened, don't you?'

When Dipak was about ten years old and Josna was already married my parents tried to find him a wife. He systematically refused them all. He always found something to hold against them: one was too dark skinned, another wasn't pretty enough, another was illiterate, still another was taller than he was and so on. Our parents finally threw in the towel, and tough luck if the dowry would be less than they had expected. Why don't they treat me the same way? Is it because I am a girl and a potential risk to the family honour? And even though they want to free them-selves from their responsibilities, why not wait until I finish school?

My brother Dipak is very understanding. He always supported me when the chance of going to school came up. When I don't study enough or my marks are a little less good he orders me to work harder, to do my homework more seriously. He advises me to read and to have a look at the lessons of the curriculum before the information is brought up by my teachers. He himself is sorry not to have continued at school for longer. He gave it up around the age of twelve to begin – like all of us – to earn money. However, I can see that he is unhappy with his job because he is not cut out for physical work; on the other hand he is blessed with a very quick mind. Some years later he regrets what he did. The tea stall brings in a little to help the family, but not enough to start a family of his own. It's thanks to him that we have been able to put electricity in the house. He pays the bills so that my parents can devote their income to buying food.

That evening he advises me to stay with our uncle. There's

no point starting the conflict up again by going back home, since my mother is probably still furious. I agree with him. He promises to bring me my school things early the next morning.

It is after eight o'clock, and I've been up for nearly two hours. Dipak is late in coming, and I'm going to be late to school. I go to the house hoping that Ma will be away. I see her in the court-yard weaving bamboo baskets. She sees me and looks daggers at me. Her dark, piercing eyes are fierce, her lips pursed. Dipak takes me by the hand and tells me that my mother no longer wants me to go to school. Her decision is final, and neither he nor Baba has succeeded in making her change her mind. She will not tell me directly because she has sworn not to speak to me again.

All right then. I go back into the room, grab the tobacco basket and go plonk myself down at the other end of the courtyard near Budhimuni's house. In one morning I make more than five hundred cigarettes. I have so much experience that I can work with my eyes closed. If I keep on at this rate, in no time I'll beat my father's production figure of a thousand bidis a day. There is also a high probability that my back will be wrecked and my fingers bent before I'm married. And it's not impossible that my mother and I will never speak to each other again.

I hear the children chattering in the street, and I recognize the voices of Budhimuni, Ashok, Pinky and the others. Atul asked them to find out why I haven't been to school. I reply briefly that I had to drop everything and help my parents. The conversation very quickly turns to the newspaper articles that

all the parents in the village are talking about. I really under-
estimated the impact of my speech. I am under no illusion now
that the whole country knows about my talk. Budhimuni is
the only one who understands the extent of the damage. She
advises me to talk about it with the teachers at the school. For
the time being I don't want to make the situation worse, even
though she is undoubtedly basically right – but I have no idea
how to get out of this mess I've created. I ask her to lie to Atul
and Arjun and tell them that I had to go to my sister's in
Sampur. I don't want to get them mixed up in this business. I
have already hurt my family enough by giving them so much
bad publicity.

Baba dismisses the children who are clustered around me.
He is livid. He confirms what Dipak told me before with regard
to the school. From now on my main activity will consist of
either making bidis or else going to the brick factory where my
sister works. I reply calmly that I prefer to follow his line of
work because I don't feel like learning a new trade.

'Tomorrow we will go to the dealer to get double the
amount of tobacco and eucalyptus leaves,' he says with finality.

Several days went by, but my mother didn't get over the shock-
wave that I caused in the press. She spent a lot of time squatting
in the courtyard brooding over the shame that I had brought on
our family. She didn't open her mouth except to insult me. She
told me that from now on she would no longer feed me, that
she was going to make my life so difficult and unbearable that
I was soon going to look back longingly at the time now gone
by when she loved me with all her heart. So that she would be

certain not to come face to face with me she wove her baskets in the neighbouring courtyard with the other women.

I took advantage of the fact that she wasn't watching me to go for a walk down the main street. I couldn't take a step in the village without hearing remarks or being asked questions about my speech. I brushed off those remarks and claimed that it was nothing to do with me, that there had been a mistake. Most of the people had only a very vague idea of what had been said. Nobody had really read the newspapers. I found it strange that my neighbours were interested more in my marriage than in me myself.

At home I tried to redeem myself by bringing in some extra income to supplement my father's. I worked all day without a break. In the evening, at dinnertime, my mother forbade me to enter the house. I stretched out under the little window where I shivered with the cold. Dipak discreetly brought me a small portion of rice, which I devoured in a few seconds. I waited until everyone was asleep to sneak indoors without making any noise.

I was woken up by kicks, blows with a stick and insults from my mother.

'Get out of here, you little bitch! Who told you you could sleep inside? Clear off! You worthless brat! You dishonour your whole family, but you still want to take advantage of its generosity and its hospitality. Who fed you from her own breast when you were only an infant? You want to make decisions by yourself, eh? In that case, you will never sleep under our roof again!'

I ran out of the house, shielding my head from a possible blow from a bamboo stick. Once I got to the well I stopped, out of breath. I poured some water over my head. My hand was injured, and the least movement of my wrist was terribly painful.

This treatment went on for several weeks, and if I succeeded in coping with this domestic violence it was above all because my father's attitude had softened. He regularly had me sent some little helpings of food when my mother wasn't around. Dipak brought me a straw mattress and a little blanket so that I wouldn't die of the cold when I spent the night out of doors. Sometimes I thought that it would be better if I went to live for a while with my sister to escape the hell that my mother was making me live in, but I had to forget about that because it was quite possible that her in-laws would throw me out even before I got to the doorstep.

I recognize the voice of my teacher Atul. He is asking why I haven't come to school for weeks. My mother answers him in a friendly tone of voice and says that I am with my elder sister and that for economic reasons I had to take a job in that district. Atul insists that I must return to school as soon as possible. Many concepts have been dealt with in the course of these last weeks that I absolutely must catch up with before it is too late. My mother answers, still in a friendly tone of voice, that she will pass the message on to me as soon as we speak on the phone or when she goes to Sampur, adding that I really don't wish to go on with my schooling any more. She is lying through her teeth. I don't know how long I can keep resisting this pressure and coping with this situation. I know that everything would go back to normal if only I would accept the marriage proposition.

Back in the courtyard I see my mother with a stick. I push the tobacco basket away and try to escape, but it's too late. She slaps me and the cigarettes go flying in all directions. I rub my jaw as I gather up the leaves. She grabs me by the arm, drags me inside the house and closes the door.

8

TRAINING

It was damp. The sky was overcast, and a storm was on its way. In the distance I could already hear the rumbling of thunder. My body and my stomach understood that they had to be satisfied with a few balls of rice per day. My legs were covered with bruises, my face was puffy and I had a backache from rolling bidis from dawn to dusk. However, these discomforts and the treatment inflicted by my mother seemed to be relatively less dramatic than what my sister had endured.

I set myself up in a small space on the dried-mud terrace running out from our house. The last few nights had been especially chilly; winter was coming. I asked Dipak to get me a sheet to cover myself in the evening. At every moment of the day I kept looking around for fear that my mother would suddenly appear. Her insults and bullying always led to slaps or blows with a stick. Her anger seemed permanent and sometimes plunged her into an alarming state. I had the impression that my decision terrified her. Unlike Ma the village neighbours had moved on to other things and even though they all still had their various opinions about it my speech was now ancient history.

The arguments inside the house got worse. Dipak was angry with Ma and reproached her for her behaviour the day before when I repeated my wish not to be married. Baba intervened and also defended me. Ma didn't want to hear about it. As long as she lived her children would submit to the rules, which had proved to be well founded. She accused them of being 'cowardly', of being 'irresponsible', of 'letting me play and waste my time at school when we have nothing to eat'. My brother pointed out to her that Josna had nearly died four times because of these outdated rules. Voices were raised, the tone became heated. Dipak announced that he was going to leave the village to try his luck in a big city – Calcutta or Bangalore. His mind was made up; he didn't want to stay in this backwater any more where there wasn't enough work.

I talked regularly to my sister on the phone, but always secretly. She had, of course, learned that I was opposed to marriage, that I had exposed our life for all to see and that since then our mother has been treating me like an animal. She took in my news, asked if the situation in the house had improved; I replied in the negative, and I apologized for mentioning her difficult pregnancies in public. She advised me not to give in to the marriage propositions, even though she was probably more afraid of our mother than I was. She envied my courage, the courage that she hadn't had when the same situation had occurred some years before. She regretted that she couldn't have any more children since her reproductive organs were so damaged. The doctor advised her to have a new operation to avoid the risk of infection in the future. Neither she nor her husband had the means to pay for the surgery just then. Her husband still didn't earn very much. I was sorry for her, for him and for their child. I asked for news about little Debu. I missed him terribly. Josna advised me just to grin and bear it and avoid any new confrontation with Ma until the tension went back down and stayed down. I could hardly believe that that was ever going to happen.

I hung up, put the telephone back in its cloth case, then put it back where it belonged among Baba's things. Then I crept into the courtyard where I had left the materials for rolling the bidis.

All three of them have come: the teacher, the headmaster of the school and the deputy minister of labour. They want to speak to my parents. The situation has gone on for too long, and some pupils have reported the bad treatment that I suffer at home. I am afraid of a new bout of anger from my mother because I'll get the worst of it as soon as they're gone. They sit down on a bed of woven rope. Baba is ashamed of receiving them without even being able to serve them a cup of *chai*. That's the reason that we receive almost no one at home. The only thing my family can offer visitors is a glass of water. Ma, who nevertheless wants to make a good impression, asks the merchant over the road to bring us some tea. She pays him with a crumpled note that she had stowed away in her bosom under her sari.

The tone of the conversation is calm and restrained, but I can't make out what they're saying. I slip into an alleyway, circle around behind the house and squeeze up against our neighbours' hut. The teacher and the headmaster say hardly anything; it's essentially the deputy minister who converses with my parents, while they sit quietly listening to him.

'You must let your daughter come back to school. It's very important for her . . .'

'It's out of the question,' Ma answers sharply. 'She has humiliated us in front of the whole village. She is the only girl to oppose marriage, all the neighbours – everyone around us –

thinks we are parents who are incapable of exercising authority over their children, even when it is a girl . . .'

'The news in the papers comes and goes. You mustn't worry about it, it is going to settle down, and in a few weeks everyone will have forgotten this story . . .'

'Where does she get these ideas? No other Kalindi is this stubborn and obstinate!'

'Your daughter is very gifted, and neither Atul, her teacher, nor Arjun, her headmaster, will contradict me. Isn't that right?'

Atul suddenly sits up, as though taken by surprise in his thoughts; he puts down the glass of tea and strokes his fine moustache to clear away the traces of liquid.

'She is an excellent pupil. She understands much more quickly than her classmates, and she is conscientious. Her home-work is always done, she often recites in class and, even if she has a tendency to act up at times, her progress is very encouraging. It is really a pity to prevent her from continuing her schooling. Children with this temperament are rare.'

'The syllabus that she is following is meant for children who have begun school late. They are supposed to do the programme in four years, but I can assure you that for your daughter it will be shorter,' the headmaster confirms. He takes off his glasses and adds, 'She is very mature; she evidently has much wider experience than her other schoolmates.'

'That's because we have taught her to work very young,' Ma says quickly. 'She began in the rice paddies, but she also knows how to roll cigarettes almost as well as her father, and from the earliest age she has helped me do housework and look after her brothers and sisters. She will be a perfect wife, especially at this age when girls are most in demand.'

'That's all very well, but it is a very short-term view. Every day at the Ministry of Labour we have thousands of children who give up school to help their parents. Hundreds of children are married without their consent and in our experience all of them without exception give up school. And again I'm only talking about reported cases, the ones that have come to our attention. The reality is much worse.'

Baba seemed reassured to know that our situation and our poverty were not exceptional cases, at least much less so than he thought. No one really likes to admit that he scrapes along in very precarious conditions.

'Your daughter has outstanding potential. She speaks well. I have seen her give a speech in front of hundreds of people without having stage fright, and the reactions were excellent. There are very few children capable of doing that without having had a lengthy preparation beforehand. You should not treat her as you are doing . . .'

Baba listened conscientiously to the three officials. He was proud that these important people were talking about his daughter in these terms.

'Furthermore,' continued Mr Kundu, 'the treatment that you're inflicting on her is against the law, as you well know. And there's a very good chance that the village *panchayat* will turn against you.'

'The *panchayat* has never prevented anyone from getting married, as far as I know. Look at all our neighbours. They do the same thing; there is nothing wrong with that. And then your speeches are very fine, but the fact is that in the end I still have nothing to put on the children's plates,' Ma exclaims.

'And that's the reason that you refuse to feed her and that you hit her?' the headmaster replies drily.

'We take care of our daughter the same as we do our other children,' my mother retorts.

I jump out from my hiding place. 'That's not true! She's lying! For weeks now she's been hitting me every day. She insults me, and she won't give me any food. I'm not even allowed to sleep indoors. Would you like me to show you where I spend my nights?'

My intervention surprised everyone. Silence. My father was embarrassed, and if it weren't for the presence of the men my mother would have strangled me with her bare hands for defying her in this way – and in front of strangers.

'She's exaggerating. It's her fiery temperament. Sometimes I can't help thinking that she's possessed by demons.'

'It's you who are raving mad. I work day and night. I go get wood in the forest. I carry water from the river. I agreed to roll cigarettes full-time so that we could have some new income. And in spite of that you keep trying to impose a marriage on me that I don't want to hear about. As long as I don't give in – and I will not give in – you treat me the way a mother-in-law treats her daughter-in-law, and that is like a slave. In front of these gentlemen you dare to assume the role of the kindly and protective mother?'

My mother railed in the face of this affront, made all the worse by the presence of strangers. Before the situation deteriorated further, the deputy minister took matters in hand by ordering me to let the adults speak among themselves. I didn't argue. I knew that they had heard me and that they understood. I obeyed, glad to have told the truth in front of them.

'Is that the reason you want to marry her off? To have one less mouth to feed?' asked Mr Kundu.

'Yes, among others,' Baba replied. 'There is also the price of the dowry. At her age that should work out at about five thousand rupees, but in a few years, when she is older, we will have to lay out much more. I don't have the means to wait for her to finish her schooling. And anyway there is nothing so awful about wanting to get one's children married. I married my wife when she was even younger that Rekha. And it was my father who decided for me.'

'If your daughter keeps on at school she will find a husband very easily, and your dowry will be minimal . . .'

'How's that?'

'We have a proposition to put to her. We want her to represent the cause of the children in this region. She has the talent and the educational standard. All she needs is some instruction so that she can channel her energy.'

'But that won't solve the financial problem. You can see for yourselves that we are poor. This mud-brick house is our only fortune. I don't even have a parcel of land to work. Every day we have to find the means to pay for the evening meal and for the next day,' Baba continued, while Ma champed at the bit but didn't dare open her mouth again.

'I can help you get an allowance from the government. There are funds reserved for families under a certain income threshold called the BPL, or Below Poverty Line. I think that you probably fulfil the criteria. If you agree that Rekha can return to school I will undertake to make the procedure easier. That can be done in a few months,' Mr Kundu said, replacing the strand of hair, aware that he had just for the first time touched a sensitive point, maybe even convinced my parents, who asked for time to think about it.

Mr Kundu left them until the next day to decide. Atul stressed how I had got behind in my schooling during the previous few weeks. Arjun recalled that it was very possible that, considering my abilities, I could do the syllabus in two or three years instead of the four as anticipated, thus opening the regular programme to me only a few years late. But to do that I must absolutely get back to my studies as soon as possible.

In spite of the late hour the light from the lantern still flickers in the black night. My parents have been talking for quite a while. Dipak joins in the conversation. I am shivering under my sheet, but strain my ears to try to catch a few words. The meeting this morning has triggered a full-on family council with, as so often in these recent times, my case as the main subject. My brother and my father are working on my mother. I hear Baba loud and clear. He pounds his fist on the table. He is in charge of this house; the final decision is his to make. Dipak seems relieved. He welcomes this shift before the situation degenerates to the point of creating serious problems in the family, especially if the officials adopt a less diplomatic approach and the authorities interfere. In India it is never a very good idea to be in trouble with the law or the police, especially if you are poor and vulnerable, but now that is the situation we're in. Ma admits that she also wants only what is best for me.

*

The next morning my brother handed me my schoolbag. I was both moved and nervous at the idea of going back to school.

The 'back to school' went better than I could have imagined. No pupil said anything unpleasant. I know that some of them had been instructed by their families not to visit me or talk to me any more. That wasn't so bad compared with what I had been through. The class went along as though nothing had happened. Only a few pupils looked at me curiously, as if they wanted to check that I really was back.

Mr Kundu waits patiently for the end of the school day. When school is out he asks me to follow him into the headmaster's office. Arjun gives up his seat to the deputy minister, who congratulates me on being back where I belong. He repeats all the good points that he remembered from my speech at the museum of natural sciences in Purulia.

'This business can seem very trying, and I don't doubt that it has been, but believe me this experience will bear good results in a few years. For the time being I need you. Would you agree to make some more speeches like that one in Purulia?'

I answer yes without even thinking about it. The official gets up from his chair, invites Arjun to sit down again, puts his hair in place again and tells me that we will see each other again very soon.

My headmaster holds out two printed sheets of paper to me. 'Learn this by heart for the end of the week,' he tells me.

The document talks about the rights of children, about the importance of school for our education, about work and the forced marriage of children. I read and reread the pages dozens of times so as to memorize them perfectly. Certain ideas seem strange to me, but others, especially the risks of pregnancy in young girls, are more familiar. I stay after school, as do other pupils who need help, to catch up on the work I've missed.

Dipak is about to leave for Bangalore. He is carrying a bag over his shoulder in which he has put some clothing. He sold off all his tea-making equipment to pay for his travel. If everything goes well he should arrive in two days in Bangalore, where an acquaintance is ready to welcome him and help him get started. They are going to share the rent until Dipak finds steady work. On the eve of his departure I hug him tight, and he promises to call regularly. On his way he will stop to say goodbye to Josna, Badhari and Debu.

The next morning when I get up he has already gone.

Mr Kundu telephones me to say that there is a training programme coming up soon. It should last four or five days at the very most, and we will be housed on the premises with about fifty other children plus the teaching staff. The meals are provided by the government of Bengal. He wants to make sure that I want to take part in it before contacting my parents.

The atmosphere at home has mellowed a bit. The relationship with Ma is always strained, but I don't ask for anything more. My parents agree that I can join the training session planned by the Department of Labour.

A bus comes to pick us up after school finishes. At the end of the trip, and after several hours on the bus we arrive at an establishment belonging to the regional government. The girls are on the first floor and the boys are on the ground floor. The dormitory is spacious enough to accommodate everybody. I put my bag down near a window. We are in the middle of a forest, and there is almost no light in the surroundings. For the first time I am going to sleep in my own bed and on a mattress.

There are several dozen of us at the table. They serve us a very hearty dinner with chicken masala, fried vegetables and lentils, all accompanied by rotis. Mr Kundu speaks, and although we are all a bit tired from the hours of travelling we have to introduce ourselves briefly one by one. He explains to us that during these next few days we will have several exercises to do. They all have the aim of developing our leadership skills. He explains that we have been chosen from among hundreds of pupils and that he is counting on us to be up to it.

Around four in the morning we were awakened by the housemother. The first exercise consisted of dividing up into groups of six. The document that I had to learn was written on several blackboards. A teacher took each of the groups. They explained that one among us had to stand with his or her back to the board and recite the text to the others. The others had to verify that there were no errors, and if there was one they had to interrupt – but without correcting the pupil, who had to find and correct the error themselves. We all knew our text by heart, but to reel it off in front of five pairs of eyes scrutinizing the slightest misstep was a more complicated exercise than I had thought. I had to have two tries at it.

Each of the children then had to introduce themselves say the rest of the group, say where they came from and telling a little about his or her life before enrolling in school. We discovered that we had all come more or less by the same route and had the same problems. We came from poor and rural families. We had all at one time or another worked to help out family members. We had been confronted by parents who wanted us to give up school for economic reasons or for a forced marriage. It was rather comforting to realize that our case wasn't isolated and that we had much in common.

We form two circles around a ring placed on the ground. The kids in the first circle have big marbles; the ones at the back have normal-sized marbles. The object of the game is to push the marbles that are scattered in a random way outside the ring to inside it. For the first circle of kids it is easier because they have big marbles and are closer to the target. The teacher watches us, takes notes and referees the game. He explains to us what lesson we should take away from this .

'The kids in the first row have big marbles, which represent their potential to succeed. They have an advantage compared with the ones who are in the back, further away on the one hand, but also at a disadvantage because they have only one little marble. Now we are going to change one thing: the first circle has ordinary marbles and the second has big marbles. Now, take your places again.'

We notice that it is possible to push the marbles into the ring even when you are at a distance. I understand the principle: it doesn't matter much whether you are in front or behind, what counts is to have a bigger marble.

'Poor people are the second circle, the better-off people are the first circle. And as I told you before your potential lies only in what you have in your hand. You have noticed that you can succeed even when you are at a distance? Remember that the ordinary marble and the big marble represent your academic attainment. If you have a good level you will have more chances to succeed in life. It matters little where you come from.'

I am staggered by this analogy, which makes sense and which explains that even poor people like us can one day get out of poverty. I later tried hard to explain that to my parents, but they never really understood what I meant.

In a second go – still around the ring – they ask us to form teams of two: one person from the first circle and the other from the second circle. You have to communicate discreetly so as not to be blocked by the other teams. It is rather tricky to define the rules and strategies of dialogue with people you've only known for a few hours. If my friends had been there it would have been simpler. The teacher explains to us that he will go back over this game after the lunch break.

I meet several remarkable people during this workshop. Some of them have really suffered, and it seems that what links us is the fact that we've been working when other children were going to school and getting instruction. I also notice that some of us are capable of taking the initiative while others aren't at all. Each one has certain qualities, the aim being to combine them so that a team is effective. I have just understood the other point of the game of marbles.

Other activities are planned until dinner time. At the end of the day we are exhausted, and once in our dormitory we all go straight to sleep.

*

The next morning they hand out newspapers, scissors and paste. The object of the game this time is to put together a banner on which the words cut out and juxtaposed form a coherent sentence. All the groups are in competition. In the beginning you have to make a sentence with five words as fast as possible. Then it gets more and more difficult with ten or fifteen words. I understand that to win you have to get organized. I get the team together and assign everyone a role. Three are to search for words and are supposed to say them out loud so that we can see how we are going to arrange them; two are busy cutting them out and sticking them in the right order; finally the sixth should supervise the process to avoid an error slipping through. The members of our team demonstrate that this is the right strategy, for we win one game after another. To make the game more interesting, some pupils aren't allowed to make use of their arms and legs, or they are blindfolded. At each new constraint, we have to redefine the roles. The ones who are blindfolded are given the job of, for example, sticking down the words. Those who can't use their bodies read the newspaper cuttings. I like this game a lot because you constantly have to adapt yourself to new rules.

On the last day we all have to give a talk to the other pupils. Fifteen minutes before going up on the platform we are given a piece of paper with the subject that we have to talk about. We absolutely must finish in less than ten minutes and not stray from the subject. All the subjects have been treated in the course of the workshop or in the document that we had to memorize, and I get the health risks during a too-early pregnancy – a subject I'm an expert on.

*

The last half-day is devoted to a summing up. Mr Kundu congratulates us and explains how this game-playing is actually very important. Once we get back to school we will have a special role to play. To be able to play it properly we have had to develop our oral skills and sense of leadership and make sure we are completely up to date on the rights of children. Before speaking in public we must be sure we have a simple and clear message to communicate, go right to the heart of the matter, master our elocution and the pace of our speech and remember to make use of examples – ideally our own experiences – to increase the credibility of our presentation.

Mr Kundu reminds us that the teaching team is always at our disposal if we need advice or supplementary information. He asks us never to forget that we are different from other kids and that our influence can make things change.

9
PLEA

After my speech at the museum a few journalists followed the development of my situation. The interest they took in my story encouraged me in my ideas and my fight. I also received the support of several politicians. In concrete terms that materialized in small donations of money or of goods, chiefly for the practical difficulties of daily life.

A team of reporters came from abroad especially to meet me, and they spent several days in the village. I introduced them to my friends and schoolmates as well as my teachers. They stayed for quite a while talking with my parents.

On the last day we went to the big weekly market at Sampur. Josna, her husband Badhari and Debu came with us. We came back laden with shopping bags: vegetables, a chicken, spices, rice and lentils. There had never been so much food in the house. The reporters insisted that we also buy some cooking utensils, cleaning materials, new mattresses and some blankets for winter. My brother-in-law Badhari was astounded at the sight of a brushed metal razor with interchangeable blades and a soft shaving-brush. The journalists gave it to him, and he promised to keep it for years.

A little before their departure the cameraman handed me some cash. I promised him I would spend it suitably. I asked the advice of my teacher, who suggested that I enrol in a training course in computing – the only subject that we don't study at all in school because we don't have the equipment.

The little room was nicely arranged. Computers equipped with a webcam were placed in a semicircle. A ceiling fan stirred the cool air blown out of the air conditioner. Just above the office of the owners a big framed portrait of Sai Baba – a figure revered by both Hindus and Muslims – looked down on the room.

Two brothers who had spent most of their time in Calcutta set themselves up in an out-of-the-way spot near their native village to be closer to their parents. They were Muslim and knew all about computers. I signed up for their training course with my friend Budhimuni. The courses took place whenever one wished over a period of three months.

Yusuf showed us how to use computers to listen to music, watch films or even access the internet. We were taught the basics of office computer programs: we learned to create or open a text document, to write and to save. I find the word-processing program very easy to use and very practical, even if I often make mistakes. When there was a power cut the brothers started up the generator, and the computers came to life again. Each time we got to grips with a new concept we moved on to another. These machines contained tons of secrets – and even if we devoted all our time to it we would always have something more to learn. Yusuf was happy to pass on his knowledge: he seemed to have mastered computing to perfection. His explanations were very clear, and he didn't hesitate to make comparisons with daily life so that we would understand better.

The trip home took an hour on foot. My parents insisted that I never come back at night. I suggested buying a bicycle with the money we had been given by one of the politicians. That would be useful for everybody and make the longest trips easier. Baba approved of this idea, and we went together to Purulia by bus. We met my brother-in-law. He advised us to go to see his boss, who had several hundred bicycles and would have some good advice.

Gopal Babu was in his workshop supervising dozens of people who were repairing things, hammering things or inflating the tyres of the vehicles that were fairly bashed up from their intensive use. The racket was deafening. At the back of the yard two men were welding a passenger seat on to a rickshaw. On the left a dozen workers were handling and daubing some parts covered with grease in plastic basins whose colour you could hardly make out. Their fingers were black and sticky, and the grease had got under their fingernails. While Baba was introducing himself and the owner was listening absent-mindedly I noticed that there were several scars on his arms. He was keeping an eye on his workers. We had the feeling we were a bother and making him waste his time. His right hand didn't move but the left stroked his white beard; then he looked at his watch.

'It's nearly lunchtime. Have you eaten?'

'That's very kind of you, but we don't have much time. We're going . . .'

'If you don't take the time to eat you must really be rushed for time. But allow me to insist. You are from Badhari's family and I can't let you go away with an empty stomach. What's more the workers are about to stop, and we can talk in peace.'

'Thank you! We accept with great pleasure and thank you for your welcome and for your hospitality.'

Several little dishes were placed on a straw mat right on the ground. Squatting down we all took some vegetables, chicken, sauce and roti. Between mouthfuls Gopal Babu asked Baba, 'What exactly are you looking for?'

'We need a little bicycle. We live in Bararola and my daughter needs a bike to get to school.'

'You're looking for a bike for your daughter or for the whole family?'

'For the whole family, of course. Who can afford the luxury of having several bikes in one family?'

'There are some. Believe me, there are some. When I was a boy there weren't many cycles, but as time went on some people got rich, and the bike is still the most affordable way to get around. Your daughter goes to school, you say? That is a very good thing. Me, I fought for my children to be able to have an education worthy of the name and have an easier trade than mine. They are all in the United States and come back to see me every summer. They have their problems, too, but then everybody has problems, right?'

'Yes, life isn't easy, but it is our destiny to follow the route ordained by the gods.'

'Without wishing to sound like a blasphemer, I have learned in the course of my modest life that the gods are also open to negotiation. Their judgement is not as final as people think,' Gopal Babu replied, before bursting out laughing.

Baba didn't react. I smiled and, for fear of being observed, I bowed my head over my plate.

'What do you do for a living, Kalindi? You're a farmer?'

'No, I have no land, unfortunately. I roll bidis.'

'That gets very painful after a while, they tell me . . .'

'I'm not complaining! After twenty years it's true that my back hurts, but the advantage is that I have completely stopped smoking.'

'That's a good thing! And is your daughter doing well at school?'

'Yes, she spends her time studying, nothing else interests her . . .'

'That's good, my girl,' says Gopal, fixing me with his dark eyes. 'You have to take advantage of these carefree moments to work and think about your future. My children are very glad that I urged them to go to university rather than to work as cycle-rickshaw drivers. I can't help feeling I've seen you before . . . Have we already met?'

'I don't think so, Sir, or I would have remembered it.'

'Wait a minute, you aren't Rekha? The little girl in the newspapers?'

'Yes, my name is Rekha . . .'

I felt that my father was uncomfortable at this turn of the conversation.

'Oh, yes. I remember. You're the little girl who refuses to get married!'

Babu went pale; he thought that this story was buried for good, but it had followed him here.

'Listen, Karno, daughters like yours are exceptional. I am

delighted to meet you. I don't know what other people say to you, but I want you to know that I am very proud to meet you. You must get a lot of rude remarks, especially in your village, but you will always have my support. Our country needs people like you. I had three sons, but if I had had a daughter I would have given her the same chances as her brothers.'

'Thank you for your support, Gopal. We're very happy to have a daughter with so much character and personality.'

'Enough of this chit-chat! Amosh, go to the workshop, take the best bike, service it, lubricate it properly and bring it here when it's ready.' Gopal ordered one of his workers, who hurried off towards the garage.

'This is very kind of you, Gopal Babu, but I am determined to pay.'

'I understand. Even if my gesture is not out of charity, I don't want to offend you. Give me what you had in mind in budgeting for the bicycle, and if you have the least problem come back to see me. This bike is "guaranteed", as all the companies say nowadays who sell fans or mixers,' he said, bursting out again with a deep laugh.

'Thank you very much! May the gods reward you for your goodness,' Baba stammered while holding out the carefully folded notes.

The owner put them in his pocket without counting them. Amosh returned a few minutes later accompanied by a magnificent black bicycle with a leather saddle, new tyres, a basket on the handlebars and a luggage carrier equipped with a cushion. I was thrilled, although the machine was almost as high as I was, and it looked like I was going to have trouble riding it by myself.

We set off for the village after thanking Gopal Babu at length for lunch and for giving us such a good price on the bike.

We glided along the road, the breeze whipped against my face, the wind blew through my hair. I was sitting sideways on the comfortable luggage carrier. My father pedalled faster and faster under a glorious sun. When we reached the statue of Hanuman we got off the bike so that we wouldn't damage the tyres by riding over sharp stones. When we were on the dirt track again Baba suggested that I pedal the bike. I was impatient to take over the machine, and I pedalled fast, the better to feel the cool wind on my cheeks.

In our excitement we forgot to buy a padlock so the bicycle had to spend the night inside the house.

I have been appointed the head of the class. Atul announces it to the pupils at the end of the school day. If a tricky problem comes up or if we have questions that we prefer to deal with among ourselves the pupils can come to see me. On the way home my friends congratulate me and are curious to know what my training programme was all about. I tell them that we played games while learning a lot of things, that I met people with the same problems that we have even though they live a long way away from our school.

I don't go into the details because I have to call my sister. She is confined to bed with a fever, and her voice on the telephone is weaker than usual. The doctor prescribed her some tablets to lower her temperature. I ask her if she is carrying a new baby in her belly. She says she's not – at least she doesn't think she's pregnant. Spontaneously I suggest paying for the operation that the doctor has been advising her to have for some months.

The next day I accompany my father to the bank to withdraw the last few thousand rupees that remain in my account. He gets on the bus to the in-law family, and I ride the bike back home. Mr Kundu tells me that he has just organized the first session at which I must speak in public. That's in one week, but I don't mention it to my parents.

After school the headmaster and the deputy minister of labour are waiting for me so that we can go together to the meeting place. When we get there several dozen people are waiting. The meeting is taking place in front of the police station in Jalda, several kilometres from our house.

Mr Kundu takes the floor to explain why we are there today. 'For several years we have been running a programme to combat child labour. We have been studying the problems parents encounter in nourishing your offspring. We have noticed that if very young children work it is mainly to help their families. But we have also noticed that they work because they have quit school. Now, schooling is obligatory, and no one is exempt from it. The prime minister has again reminded us of that in her speech.'

The crowd listens, and some idle onlookers come along, prick up their ears and ask what it's all about. The children – both boys and girls – are placed in front, just opposite the lectern. A piercing whistling accompanies the words coming out of the loudspeakers, but I hear my name, and I can see Mr Kundu making a sign for me to come up.

'This girl is like you! You could be her parents, and today she is here to tell you her story. Rekha, please come and introduce yourself.'

I am impressed by the crowd below the platform. All eyes are fixed on me. I have a lump in my throat, and I'm afraid of stammering. However, as soon as I go up to the microphone the nervousness disappears and my delivery is clear.

'My name is Rekha Kalindi, and I come from the village of Bararola. Ever since I was very little I've worked to help my parents, who are very poor. There are six children in the family. On the days when we have nothing to eat we go to bed with empty stomachs and hope that the next day will be better. When my parents decided that I ought to be married I refused.'

I pause for a moment. The crowd is hanging on my every word. Some of them are surprised by my last sentence. They are doubtless astonished that someone can question parental views when she is still a child – all the more so to do it in a public place.

I continue, 'But let me tell you what happened to my older sister. For five years she tried to have a baby. Every time she gave birth she nearly died. Her cries, her pains, were heart-rending. She escaped death several times but not the sorrow of losing four babies. My sister did not choose to marry, but my parents chose for her. They decided that she was mature enough to be married and young enough for the dowry to be minimal. I am not criticizing my parents. They do their best every day to put a bit of rice on our plates. On the other hand I do not agree with their forcing me to quit school and marry a stranger older than I am just to have one fewer mouth to feed. That was not easy. I would even say that it is extremely difficult to contradict one's parents and the consequences are especially hard to take. But today I am here to tell you that it is possible to refuse a marriage if you don't want it. It is possible to find another way that allows you to go to school so that you can really help your parents, have a life less hard than theirs and give your children better living conditions than the ones you had. It is an ambitious vision that is within the reach of each of you. Thank you for listening to me.'

I had hardly finished my last sentence when the crowd began to applaud, mainly the young people in the first row. Mr Kundu took the floor again and reminded everyone that the law forbids boys to marry before the age of twenty-one and girls before eighteen.

I went back down from the platform, happy to have expressed myself in front of all these people, proud of having shared my story, delighted at the idea that it could inspire other people in the same situation.

At the end of the meeting several pupils came up to confide their problems to me. Dipali was twelve, and although her parents wanted to keep sending her to school she was being forced to marry a man of about twenty because her grandfather absolutely had to see her married before he died. I advised her to ask her grandfather if he preferred to go first or to attend the funeral of his granddaughter because of a pregnancy that turned out to be fatal at her young age.

The case of Bina, aged thirteen, was very similar to mine. I could only encourage her to follow my example by wishing her great determination and fewer problems than those that I have had with my mother. I added that sooner or later the parents, who know they are in the wrong, realize they have no choice but to throw in the towel. With time and the support of her teachers Bina would finally succeed in convincing her parents that their decision was unworkable.

Some parents also came to greet me. Some mothers said they envied the courage they failed to have some years before; others were moved and promised to stand up to their husbands who were considering giving their daughter away although she was still too young to become a wife. I had the feeling of serving a just and praiseworthy cause by giving this speech.

Dipak landed on his feet in Bangalore and found work as a floral decorator. His work consisted of making long garlands by weaving flowers together with a string. During the wedding season he worked straight through without a break several hours a day, seven days a week, including nights. He was regularly called by hotels or rich homeowners who wished to decorate their houses during a religious ceremony or for the birthday of their child. He lived with a friend in a tiny place at the back of a little grocery where the rent was very reasonable for the centre of a big city. My brother, however, did not have access to either water or electricity. He earned enough money to feed himself but not enough to save up and come to visit us any time soon. I asked him to tell me what the people were like and how he managed not to get lost in the middle of this urban jungle. The line went dead. He had no doubt used up all the credit. I wouldn't get my answer until the next call.

I told Baba that my big brother had called, and he was sorry to have missed him. Ma came back with several woven baskets and suggested going to sell them herself at the market rather

THE STRENGTH TO SAY NO

than leaving them with the merchant. She was convinced that she could get more for them than the handful of rupees offered by the wholesaler.

The next meeting takes place in front of a hospital also situated several kilometres from the village. There are hardly any children. Once again I have butterflies in my stomach before getting up on the platform and facing dozens of adults. I adapt my speech by saying this time that since I refused the marriage proposed by my parents my dowry is very small. Less than fifteen hundred rupees, while some time ago my parents would have had to pay out more than five thousand rupees. I don't spare any detail of my older sister's miscarriages. Some women seem touched by these events, as if they themselves had experienced them and then suppressed the memory before they surfaced again with my speech. They are the ones that I particularly address, the mothers, for although they almost never have the power to make decisions they exert a great influence on their husbands. I encourage them to listen to their daughters rather than to punish them or to bully them. I mention my painful confrontation with Ma, who is now sorry and recognizes that she was wrong. I urge these mothers not to repeat the same error as the one committed by my mother.

I speak for a little over ten minutes. The message seems to get through to judge by the reactions of the crowd. The deputy minister straightens his unruly hair before concluding and thanking the audience. I have the impression that he, too, appreciated my speech.

*

The public meetings multiplied without my really realizing it. I had to do about fifteen of them in all. The deputy minister insisted on making an evaluation after each speech. He corrected me, especially when I talked for too long. He reminded me of the points that we dealt with during the training programme. He also noted the positive elements in my speech; he stressed the pertinence of my examples and the very positive reactions of the audience. He was happy that the local press turned out for each of my speeches. Each interview I gave made me more credible and emphasized the depth of my message.

A journalist from the *Hindustan Times* questioned me for several minutes. She was interested in the smallest details and had me repeat the answers so that she could be sure she understood everything. The pages of her notebook became blacker the longer we talked. Her long black hair kept falling over her face, and she swept it back in an almost mechanical way. She looked like those women that you see in Bollywood films with very delicate features and full lips. When she spoke in Bengali there was no Hindi accent, so she must have been originally from Bengal. She wanted to know if I was taken care of financially – if I had received rewards or even gifts from politicians or other people. I told her the whole truth and she seemed to believe me.

The photographer shot after shot. When I ask to see them he shows me ones where the journalist and I appear sitting on the steps of my house, then some others where I am alone or in close-up. He asks me to roll some bidis since that's my usual work. I take the basket and the leaves, and in the space of a few minutes I show the camera twenty-five perfectly rolled cigarettes. The camera clicks away. The photographer glances at the screen, expertly turns the buttons then nods. The journalist asks him if he's satisfied, and he replies that he has enough good photos to illustrate the article.

My parents are also interviewed, first separately and then together. Even the neighbours come in for a few questions. The reporter takes my mobile, enters her number and asks me to call her if I need anything at all. I thank her politely. I can't begin to suspect that when it appears her article will be read by practically everybody in India, including the president.

The next meeting took place in Calcutta. I was told a few days beforehand, and I learned that other important people would speak. My teacher reassured me and said that I didn't need to panic or get stressed, that it would be the same routine as before with the sole difference that there would be many more people in the audience. Mr Kundu, on the other hand, pointed out to me that I had to be word perfect and more effective than ever. I didn't know which one to believe. My parents were informed, and my mother insisted that Baba came with us.

The car arrived at noon to drop us off at the railway station. The train trip seemed to go on for ever; we had time to eat lunch and dinner. Some people from the ministry accompanied us, and some of them stared at me for a long time because they'd never seen me before. When night came the train staff distributed sheets and a plastic-covered pillow to us. Somebody came to transform the seats into couchettes and in a few minutes the carriage had turned into a huge dormitory. I was just above my father. I had trouble getting to sleep with the noisy rumbling of the train.

The first rays of sunshine came through the filthy window. I got up and gazed at the landscape that was flashing past my eyes.

When we arrived several men welcomed us; they were wearing short-sleeved shirts and ties, and they drove us in a white vehicle with a revolving light on top. The interior of the car was comfortable. Mr Kundu took advantage of the drive to give me some last-minute advice: concentrate, be systematic and if there are any questions deal with them promptly.

There were several thousand people standing behind barriers, which were a few metres from the platform. Big posters were stuck on both sides of huge surrounding walls. I was invited to sit on one of the chairs on the stage. They gave me a little bottle of mineral water, and the guests arrived one after the other. The polite greetings and the hugs and kisses lasted for many minutes while the public poured in. I put my hands together and bowed my head each time someone came to greet me.

When the first speaker finally got up to speak I had already been sitting and trying to stay awake for almost two hours. On the lawn cameras were filming the scene. Sometimes a camera-man got up on the platform, went up to the politicians, recorded some images and climbed back down off the stage and rejoined his colleagues. The speeches were vehement. Some speakers shouted into the microphone enough to start up a loud whistling. Others used their hands and their fists to emphasize an idea, to get the message across. I never do that.

Some children went up on the platform, and I was called to sing with them. They put a microphone in my hands, and I started singing a Bengali song that we learned at school. The pupils followed the beat. Then I was invited to take my place at the rostrum and introduce myself. I lifted my *dupatta* so that it didn't get caught on my sandals. The audience was quiet, everyone was looking at me and the cameramen aimed their cameras at me. I felt panic mounting. No sound came out of my mouth. The crowd extended as far as the eye could see. If I didn't say something very soon the situation could get very embarrassing. I remembered that in these cases you need to start by saying something simple. So I introduced myself. The rest followed as one push of the pedal follows another. I went back over my sister's marriage at the age of twelve and her multiple disastrous pregnancies. I mentioned the health problems linked to early marriage and the risks of childbirth out in the countryside, often without medical assistance. I mentioned the fact that fertility is not 100 per cent assured at our age. I then carried on with the marriage propositions my parents had received, my refusal to go along with them, the sanctions and the pressures that I was subjected to and the slow reconciliation with Ma, who now regretted her behaviour. I mentioned the examples of other girls I met during the training programme who had given in to their parents.

'If I said no to marriage it is, as I have just told you, for reasons of health – but also to continue my schooling. I worked for a long time in the rice paddies. For a long time I helped my father produce bidis so that our family could earn a little more money. There were days without rice, days without rotis, when we had to beg for food from neighbours. They were supportive but also as destitute as we were. But there were also days at school when my schoolmates and I spent time just being children – learning rather than going to work, being instructed rather than breaking our backs or ruining our health.'

I paused. I had been speaking for nearly twenty minutes, and I needed to think about drawing to a close.

'If I refused to submit to the decisions of my parents that doesn't mean that I lack respect for them or that I have a secret boyfriend.'

The crowd laughed. I smiled and continued, 'That does not call into question their authority or their responsibility for our education. If I refused it is because I know that their choice is not theirs but that of the community, which wishes to see each little girl go to her in-law family as soon as possible, often for economic reasons. Kids – you, too, have the power to refuse to be married while you are still young. Parents – don't give in to the pressure of your family, your neighbours or friends. Allow your children to have a chance to help you concretely and significantly once their schooling is finished! Thank you for listening to me.'

I returned to my seat as the crowd applauded warmly. The politician who spoke just afterwards stressed my courage, my determination and my capacity for judgement in spite of my young age. He congratulated my parents for having given me life so that I might help other people change theirs.

According to the officials with me there were at least five thousand people in the audience. This was the first time that I had spoken in front of so many people. If at the beginning I had butterflies in my stomach and my shyness got the upper hand, I still managed to express myself clearly.

After the meeting a lot of young people wanted to meet me. One girl confided to me that she was desperate: her family had already struck a deal for her marriage, and the wedding was planned for the next month. I advised her to speak to her parents then to refuse to eat, not to take part in domestic life and, the most important thing, to stand firm. She was afraid of contradicting her parents and of being punished or thrown out of the house but promised to stand up to them. She confided to me that without my speech she would never have dared to consider taking the plunge.

10

HEROES DAY

This is the first time I've ever touched snow. The flakes brushing against my cheeks cause an electric sensation that runs up and down my spine. My face is damp, and I have never been so cold. They warned us that it would be chilly in the capital, but none of us could have imagined such low temperatures. I am dressed in so many layers of clothing that I can hardly manage to walk normally. I take several photos that I will be able to show on my return to the Bengal region. For several days I have been in New Delhi with around twenty other young people from all over the country who have come to attend Heroes Day. This event is organized by the leaders of the country to honour young people who have accomplished something significant and important for India.

The all-terrain vehicle grazed the houses. The villagers were obliged to go inside their shacks if they wanted to avoid getting run over. The narrow road was meant for carts, bikes and perhaps cars, but no one would ever have imagined that one day a four-by-four of this size would go along it. The vehicle stopped in front of our house. I climbed inside, and my mother said goodbye to me. She wondered if she hadn't done a stupid thing in allowing this trip, which was going to separate us for nearly two weeks. She put the veil of her sari over her hair, taking care to hide one eye already wet with tears. We had to go on a few hundred metres to have enough room to turn around and get back on the road out of the village. We got to the station at around seven o'clock. The Rajdhani Express was going to leave in half an hour. We got on board, and I chose a compartment where there was room for my friend Afsana and my father, who was accompanying me. It was the second time that he was going to New Delhi, too. The train left on time! That was good news because it meant that we should arrive on schedule the next morning at about ten.

In the train the conversations started very quickly. Who were we? Where were we going? The passengers were surprised and delighted to learn that we were going to the capital to meet the president, the prime minister and the secretary general of the Congress Party. I was sure that they had already forgotten why we were invited, dazzled by the famous people we were going to meet. The further the train went and the more travellers got on board, the more our accents became noticeable. We heard incomprehensible regional languages being spoken. When night fell we got into our couchettes.

I woke up early in the morning when the WCs were free and the carriage was still asleep. I washed and got dressed quickly and then I went back and sat on the couchette. Waiting while the other passengers surfaced one after the other I watched the scenery go by.

In recent months I had travelled around to dozens of villages and met several thousand people thanks to my public speeches. If the schools and public places in general accorded me a favourable reception that was not always the case with certain committees in villages where the traditions were more entrenched. I remember the mother who tried to hit me because I was spreading unhealthy ideas in the minds of her daughters. According to her I was spreading ideas that were unworthy, insulting and degrading for our society. Like my mother she thought that if the young children now had the right to see and approve of their future husbands they would go off the first chance they got and lose their virtue. I had trouble explaining that the health risks could be critical. She didn't want to hear about it, replying that she herself had given birth to six children without ever feeling she was at death's door. Her daughter was neither more nor less fragile, so why should she give up on finding a husband soon?

It was obvious that this woman had never had any miscarriages or a stillborn baby and that she was unaware of the risks that she was making her daughter run. The public was divided on the question. The debate was launched. Each of us stuck to our position. For the first time I had to make an unplanned exit before the situation got out of control. There is no one more deaf than the one who doesn't want to hear.

I also remember the father who violently took me to task during another speech. He accused me of being ignorant of our traditions and of corrupting minds while making poor people like them feel guilty. In uniting their children at an early age the parents were acting in their roles as unifiers of dynasties and guardians of the patronymic line. He added that marriage was something too serious to be entrusted to children. These sometimes painful confrontations were very instructive, since they helped me ponder the relevance and the meaning of the fight that I was leading.

*

My friend Afsana opens an eye. She is sitting and watching the snowflakes fall. In a few hours we will be in New Delhi. The first vendors come on board the train. In some stations there are dozens of them offering tea, coffee, fruits, rice or lentils. They bring a little thali to us, but I eat very little. The food is greasy, and there is no bread. I ask Baba if I can have some fruit and almonds. He calls out to one of the vendors, who has nothing but hot drinks. But, never mind, the seller sends his son to look for the right things so as not to lose the sale. The young man comes back a few minutes later with some peeled fruit wrapped in newspaper neatly tied with a little string. Baba takes out some rupees and hands them to the little boy who hurries to pass them on to his papa. He smiles at me. I lower my eyes, and I can't help thinking that he would be better off being in school.

We enter the New Delhi station about an hour late, but some people are there to welcome us at the end of the platform. They are bundled up in thick overcoats, and I envy them because I am freezing. They suggest going to the market to buy some warm clothing for us. From the car I see several people sitting in front of a little fire and rubbing their hands together and staying quite close to the flames. I choose a thick sweater that I put on immediately, plus a jacket and a black hat. Afsana and I are now dressed to face the winter temperatures of the capital. We go to the hotel in the car that has been assigned to us.

At the hotel I am afraid to take the lift. I admit to not trusting these big grey metal cages. I prefer to take the stairs even if our rooms are on the fourth floor. The telephone rings, and I have trouble fishing my mobile out from all the layers of clothing I have on. The number that comes up is unfamiliar, but the town code is that of Bangalore. I have just missed a phone call from my brother. A few seconds later the phone vibrates again, and I pick it up.

'Rekha? Are you all right?'

'Dipak? Yes, we're fine. We're in New Delhi!'

'In New Delhi? What are you doing there?'

'We've been invited by the president and the prime minister. They want to give us a medal. We've been selected by the "Child Heroes" programme,' I answer excitedly while getting out of my jacket and my shoes.

'But that's fantastic news. Do you know what they've planned? Do you think you'll get some money?'

'I don't know. They told us that we're going to spend a fortnight here with other kids who come from all the states of India. Baba is with me, and we're sharing a hotel room. Ma stayed in the village.'

'Was that all right with her?'

'Yes, the situation has become bearable. You know she attends meetings and says publicly that she's proud of me – that I was right to refuse the marriage propositions.'

'What? Really?'

'Yes, no kidding. At the end of one speech some girls questioned her and even congratulated her. She was happy to have all the attention. She told the pupils that she had only done her duty as a mother, that she had no other choice, considering our financial situation, but that now she is sorry she was so strict with me. I even heard her tell some pupils that she'd been wrong to be stubborn on this point.'

'She's really unpredictable. I'm glad the situation has calmed down. Tell her that I called the next time you talk to her.'

'OK, I will. You're still working as a floral decorator?'

'No, the marriage season is over. I've found a new job.'

'Oh yes?'

'Yes, I'm working in construction. I'm a builder and painter. There's a lot of work in this line. They're putting up new buildings every day here. It's exhausting, but the wages are better.'

'When are you coming to see us? It's been a long time since you came back to the village.'

'Not for six months. I'll come to see you during the next monsoon when there won't be any more work here.'

He asks to speak to Baba before the phone runs out of credit. I unpack my things while they chat for a moment.

I would have liked my brother to become a teacher. It's true that it's not paid very well, but there are several advantages to teaching in one's own village. You don't have to move house, you stay near your family and you can easily look after them in case there's a problem. The work is very interesting and instructive, on top of which you profit from a certain prestige that benefits the whole family. Instead of that Dipak goes from one hard manual job to another. Now it's impossible for him to move in another direction. Baba rings off and hands me the phone. I'm happy that he's here. He watches over me and prevents unfounded rumours from circulating. My mother and my family would never stand for anybody being able to call into question my modesty nor sullying my honour by spreading doubts about my virginity because I am far from home or because I am rubbing shoulders with strangers who could take advantage of the situation. A girl, even a poor one, is duty-bound in all circumstances to stay far from men and to be sure to avoid any compromising situation.

*

At the end of the afternoon we are all invited into the hotel lobby. They inform us that a series of activities is planned for this fortnight and that we must wear the uniform on each official outing. We are issued with a dark-red jacket featuring the national coat of arms, a pair of matching trousers, two pairs of socks and a pair of black lace-up shoes. We are invited to get acquainted with each other and to use this first evening to rest after our trip. I have trouble getting my head around the fact that we all come from the same country. Some boys wear turbans, some girls wear bracelets up to their shoulders. I later learn that the girls come from the region of Rajasthan in the far west of the country. One kid of about ten has slanting eyes and thick black hair. He looks Chinese, although his parents live in Assam. It took him more than two days to get to New Delhi by train. I am immediately faced with the language barrier. His dialect is completely strange to me, and the same for the girl with the bracelets. Afsana tells me that they are speaking their regional language just as we speak Bengali. She nevertheless manages to exchange some remarks with them in Hindi. I ask her to translate what they are saying to each other.

The girl saved several people from drowning. The ferry was crossing a branch of a river when she saw water coming in at the back of the boat. She at once warned the captain, who turned back to the riverbank where he had just weighed anchor. Without her intervention the boat would have sunk, and hundreds of people would have been drowned. In Rajasthan, as in Bengal, people rarely know how to swim.

The young boy was at the market with his mother. He noticed a man who was parking his motorbike on the pavement without bothering to untie the two big bags on the luggage carrier. He immediately thought that it could be an explosive device because a few months before that a bomb had destroyed a market, causing the deaths of several dozen people. Since then the police had called for increased vigilance. He told his mother, but she didn't believe him. The boy, who must be three or four years younger than I, then shouted, 'Bomb alert!' in the middle of the bazaar. Some men ran to him and he pointed at the motorbike and said that a man had just parked it a few minutes ago before rushing off. The market was evacuated and the police took over. A squad of bomb-disposal experts confirmed that the bag contained explosives. He was invited to meet the inspector general of the police, who suggested that he should be included in the annual Day of Young Heroes of the Nation.

Each of the following days was marked by at least one meeting with the big shots of the country. We met ministers who told us again and again that our deeds were inspirations for millions of our countrymen. There were many activities planned for every day. We went to the zoo, to the amusement park, to plays and to performances of northern Indian Kathak dancing. The next day was the most important because we were due to meet the prime minister in person. We were welcomed by one of his councillors who checked that our outfits were spotless before inviting us to follow him. We were taken to a sumptuous room with walls delicately tiled with an exquisite blue-tinted mosaic. In spite of his great age the prime minister was determined to greet us individually. He gave each child a garland of flowers, putting it around each neck. He spoke slowly and listened to accounts of why we had been chosen for this annual national event. Each of us was entitled to a little thoughtful and personal word. I was impressed by his height and his knowledge. Then he sat down on a chair and reminded us that he, too, came from a very deprived background. He said that he studied by candlelight in order to discover the light of knowledge. I was enthralled by his personal journey and by his speech, which was translated for me as he spoke. We were given a watch and a clock. I was determined to say good-bye to him and thank him before he left. The guards forbade me to approach him, but he came back one last time and put his hands together and bowed his head towards me.

I try to talk with my new friends in Hindi, but the conversation is laborious. The fact is that we don't understand each other. I have to keep calling in Afsana to interpret. The security guards laugh when they hear me making such a mess of it. However, that does not prevent us from having meals at the table with other kids. On the contrary, these linguistic concoctions give rise to unpredictable discussions that make us hoot with laughter.

They told us about the programme for the following days, the most important being Republic Day when we, as well as the army, would pass in review before the president of the country. I was astonished to learn that we would ride on the back of an elephant during the parade! I talked to my father about it once we were in our room.

'I will not climb up on an elephant.'

'You say that because you're afraid, but don't worry, it's not dangerous.'

'I'm not afraid,' I said, telling a white lie. 'It's true that the idea of being seated on the back of a pachyderm does not really reassure me. But still, Baba, I can't climb up on Sri Ganesh – he's a god! And the son of Shiva! No, no, I find it insulting and degrading to put one's backside on the divinity who is supposed to remove obstacles from life – and, remember that he also represents knowledge. I would feel guilty the moment I did it.'

'I don't think you have any choice, Rekha. The parade on Republic Day includes several thousand people! It's an honour to be there. You can't offend your hosts by refusing their customs.'

'I prefer to upset human beings than a god. I'll have a word about it tomorrow with our handlers.'

'Do what you like, but I doubt if they'll make an exception for you!'

The tutor in charge didn't seem at all offended by my request. On the contrary, he found my reasoning very respectful. He suggested that I get into one of the parade vehicles just behind the elephants. That shouldn't pose a problem. I thanked him, relieved not to have to climb up on to a howdah.

It's very cold this morning. A thick fog envelopes the great boulevard in front of the presidential residence as far as the India Gate. Soldiers in flashy uniforms, musicians and military vehicles parade in front of us. The officers salute the president, who is standing on the reviewing stand. The parade comes level with the head of state and the prime minister, and I feel hugely honoured to be there. Just when I salute I have the sensation that our eyes meet in spite of the poor visibility caused by the fog.

A big party is organized two days before our departure. There is music, and we all dance. I try once more to talk to my new friends. There is some progress, but not enough for me to do without a translator. The vast size and diversity of our country hits home. I understand also that in spite of this mosaic the kids everywhere are urged to get married from a very young age – that it's not a local or regional phenomenon but indeed a national curse. The president said it during our first meeting, but I had not really taken in the full import of her words then.

Afsana snaps me out of my reverie. We have to hurry, we have an appointment for the official photo! All the young people are in their uniforms. A photographer points out the steps to us so that we can take our places, but just then a convoy of cars stops beside us. Surrounded by several bodyguards the president gets out of her car. The plan is for her to be in the picture. She comes up to me and I greet her respectfully by putting my hands together.

'Hello, Rekha. How are you?'

'Very well, Your Excellency. Thank you for your concern.' I reply naturally and politely as we have been taught by the people looking after us these last few days.

'I am lucky to meet you twice. I hadn't thought that we would see each other again so quickly.'

'I am the lucky one to meet you a second time in such a short space, Madam President.'

'Have you enjoyed your stay?'

'Oh yes, very much. I have learned so many things that I can't wait to tell my classmates!'

'What do you want to do later?'

'I don't know yet, Madam President. I would like to teach or help change things in our country, but I don't yet have a very precise idea, mainly because I don't want to have regrets if I don't manage it.'

'I am not worried about you, and your future seems to me very promising. Let's go have the photo taken now,' she says, giving me the rose in her hand.

She sits down next to me. In a few seconds we will be in the same picture.

The next day we finished our visit by going to visit the Red Fort. I was dazzled by all the lights. It looked like Diwali, the Festival of Light, even though it was the middle of January and fog covered the city. Still, I was not unhappy to return to my village in Bengal. The further the train went, the more of my heavy clothing I could take off.

My friends were impatient for me to tell them about this latest trip. They wanted to know everything right down to the smallest detail. Atul suggested rescheduling a class so that my classmates could hear about my experience in New Delhi. I described those meetings with the other young people who were dressed differently and spoke incomprehensible languages, but had identical problems to ours. Of course, I mentioned the meetings with the members of parliament, the prime minister and the president, as well as the encouragements they gave me personally. But I also described all the villagers I had encountered. The reactions were particularly lively when I started describing the glacial weather, the sumptuous monuments and the merry-go-rounds in the amusement park – where I got motion-sick. The welcome from my classmates filled me with energy. I was full of confidence and again ready to tour villages, schools and public places in order to raise the awareness of young people and their parents about the dangers of early marriage.

After school I knock on the headmaster's door. Arjun shows me a chair and gestures for me to sit down. I have one last favour to ask of him. I preach against pre-adolescent marriage, but my speeches are directed at people whose main priority is just to survive economically. For them their children's literacy is optional. The least I ask is that Arjun guarantees me that this won't happen to my own friends and family. My parents made the mistake of not enrolling me in school from the required age, but I hope now that Arjun will provide my younger brothers and sisters with schooling so that they will never have to end up in the conditions that I am denouncing.

SOME AUTHORS WE HAVE PUBLISHED

James Agee • Bella Akhmadulina • Tariq Ali • Kenneth Allsop • Alfred Andersch
Guillaume Apollinaire • Machado de Assis • Miguel Angel Asturias • Duke of Bedford
Oliver Bernard • Thomas Blackburn • Jane Bowles • Paul Bowles • Richard Bradford
Ilse, Countess von Bredow • Lenny Bruce • Finn Carling • Blaise Cendrars • Marc Chagall
Giorgio de Chirico • Uno Chiyo • Hugo Claus • Jean Cocteau • Albert Cohen
Colette • Ithell Colquhoun • Richard Corson • Benedetto Croce • Margaret Crosland
e.e. cummings • Stig Dalager • Salvador Dalí • Osamu Dazai • Anita Desai
Charles Dickens • Bernard Diederich • Fabián Dobles • William Donaldson
Autran Dourado • Yuri Druzhnikov • Lawrence Durrell • Isabelle Eberhardt
Sergei Eisenstein • Shusaku Endo • Erté • Knut Faldbakken • Ida Fink
Wolfgang George Fischer • Nicholas Freeling • Philip Freund • Carlo Emilio Gadda
Rhea Galanaki • Salvador Garmendia • Michel Gauquelin • André Gide
Natalia Ginzburg • Jean Giono • Geoffrey Gorer • William Goyen • Julien Gracq
Sue Grafton • Robert Graves • Angela Green • Julien Green • George Grosz
Barbara Hardy • H.D. • Rayner Heppenstall • David Herbert • Gustaw Herling
Hermann Hesse • Shere Hite • Stewart Home • Abdullah Hussein • King Hussein of Jordan
Ruth Inglis • Grace Ingoldby • Yasushi Inoue • Hans Henny Jahnn • Karl Jaspers
Takeshi Kaiko • Jaan Kaplinski • Anna Kavan • Yasunuri Kawabata • Nikos Kazantzakis
Orhan Kemal • Christer Kihlman • James Kirkup • Paul Klee • James Laughlin
Patricia Laurent • Violette Leduc • Lee Seung-U • Vernon Lee • József Lengyel
Robert Liddell • Francisco García Lorca • Moura Lympany • Dacia Maraini
Marcel Marceau • André Maurois • Henri Michaux • Henry Miller • Miranda Miller
Marga Minco • Yukio Mishima • Quim Monzó • Margaret Morris • Angus Wolfe Murray
Atle Næss • Gérard de Nerval • Anaïs Nin • Yoko Ono • Uri Orlev • Wendy Owen
Arto Paasilinna • Marco Pallis • Oscar Parland • Boris Pasternak • Cesare Pavese
Milorad Pavic • Octavio Paz • Mervyn Peake • Carlos Pedretti • Dame Margery Perham
Graciliano Ramos • Jeremy Reed • Rodrigo Rey Rosa • Joseph Roth • Ken Russell
Marquis de Sade • Cora Sandel • Iván Sándor • George Santayana • May Sarton
Jean-Paul Sartre • Ferdinand de Saussure • Gerald Scarfe • Albert Schweitzer
George Bernard Shaw • Isaac Bashevis Singer • Patwant Singh • Edith Sitwell
Suzanne St Albans • Stevie Smith • C.P. Snow • Bengt Söderbergh
Vladimir Soloukhin • Natsume Soseki • Muriel Spark • Gertrude Stein • Bram Stoker
August Strindberg • Rabindranath Tagore • Tambimuttu • Elisabeth Russell Taylor
Emma Tennant • Anne Tibble • Roland Topor • Miloš Urban • Anne Valery
Peter Vansittart • José J. Veiga • Tarjei Vesaas • Noel Virtue • Max Weber
Edith Wharton • William Carlos Williams • Phyllis Willmott • G. Peter Winnington
Monique Wittig • A.B. Yehoshua • Marguerite Young
Fakhar Zaman • Alexander Zinoviev • Emile Zola

 Peter Owen Publishers, 81 Ridge Road, London N8 9NP, UK
T + 44 (0)20 8350 1775 / F + 44 (0)20 8340 9488 / E info@peterowen.com
www.peterowen.com / @PeterOwenPubs
Independent publishers since 1951